ENDORSEMENT

"Brian is a generous and humble expert who has a passion for helping others. Brian's insights from his personal experiences helped me gain the right mindset and toolset for making wise decisions in an area of real estate that was new to me."

JEFF HOUSE

Founder and CEO of Canada-based Fast Forward Ventures

"Everyone is looking for an edge in their lives; Brian Tibbs has found an edge in his personal and professional life. *The Hacker Method* gives you a step-by-step guide on expanding and elevating your game."

PASHA ESFANDIARY

Managing Partner, Evoke Capital

"Brian's Hacker Method is as powerful as I've ever read in a real estate investing book. By going through his step by step strategies, you'll save yourself years of frustrations and financial mistakes. Best of all, Brian will provide you with a detailed roadmap to finally get off the hamster wheel of living month-to-month, by carefully listing real estate investing's best holy grail secrets! Finally there's a comprehensive book that gives you the tools to "hack" yourself into the wealth class of your dreams!"

CHAD BEEMAN

CEO of Signature Championship Rings & Real Estate Investor with over 300 properties

THE
H·A·CK·E·R
METHOD

THE
H·A·C·K·E·R
METHOD

The Unexpected Investor's Guide to Building Wealth
(EVEN ON LIMITED INCOME)

BRIAN TIBBS

STRONGPrint
PUBLISHING

Visit the author's website at www.theunexpectedinvestor.com
Published and distributed by STRONGPrint Publishing
Windsor, CO

Library of Congress Control Number: 2023921434

Tibbs, Brian
The HACKER Method:
The Unexpected Investor's Guide to Building Wealth (Even On Limited Income)

ISBN 978-1-962074-11-7 (Hardcover)
ISBN 978-1-962074-12-4 (Paperback)
ISBN 978-1-962074-13-1 (eBook)

I dedicate this book to my parents, Doug and Marla Tibbs. Mom, you taught me that money has a purpose far more important than just spending it on myself. Thanks for showing me that money is also supposed to build a better future and make the world a better place. Dad, you taught me to think through the details and take measured risks. Thanks for your example of staring fear in the face and forging forward with the determination to win.

CONTENTS

A QUICK BUT VITAL INTRODUCTION

I was sharing some amazing news with a good friend over lunch. I told him that our investments had grown to the point that I no longer needed to work for a paycheck and decided to retire. He stared at me blankly for a few seconds, then asked, "How old are you?" "44", I said.

With a half-frustrated, half-confused look on his face, forgetting the social taboos around talking about money, he followed with, "How much did you make as a missionary?" I didn't know the exact answer, but I knew it was small. I responded with, "Well, our first three years as volunteers we didn't make anything. Then it slowly built over the next 13 years. Probably $3,000 to $4000 per month." I later calculated that it was an average of $9.20 per hour over my sixteen-year career as a church planter. After another blank stare and a longer pause, he asked, "How did you do it? Could I do it too? Would you show me?"

As news of my retirement spread, I found myself having that same conversation over and over. After maybe the 10th such time, it appeared that people were seriously interested in learning how to escape the paycheck to paycheck life and become masters of their own financial future.

So, I took a few steps back and looked at my 25-year journey building wealth. I discovered that I was incredibly focused on maximizing every dollar I had control of. Since my income was so low, I was obsessed with either eliminating expenses I didn't need or figuring out a way to turn an expense into income. I figured out how to "hack" our family budget to work for us instead of against us.

> Then I mapped out the 5-step process to building wealth
> on any income and called it the H-A-CK-E-R Method.

Each letter in HACKER represents a fundamental part of the process that we use in our family. I'm convinced that with the right mentality and long term discipline to the HACKER steps, anyone, regardless of their current salary, can do what I did. In fact, my hope is that you can build more wealth faster by learning from my mistakes. At first I just fumbled around and figured it out over time. You have the benefit of starting with the proven plan spelled out in this book.

The five steps of the H-A-CK-E-R Method are:

H = "Hack Your Lifestyle"

In order to build serious wealth, especially on a lower income, it's imperative that you do the six lifestyle hacks I outline in the book. Even while I was doing these hacks in my life, I was able to travel the world and live a fun and exciting life. While some of these hacks focus on limiting unnecessary expenses, the most important ones focus on turning our biggest expenses into income streams.

A = "Allocation Budgeting"

The only way to build wealth is to have a plan. In the world of finance, a plan is called a budget. I know the word budget can cause a negative reaction for some. That said, the 50/40/10 budget system is the gamified way I build wealth. If you're willing to look at your budget as a game (think Monopoly), it can actually be fun and extremely lucrative.

CK = "Cash Is King Investing"

Quite simply, the surest path to building wealth is to learn the art and science of investing. Understanding the term investing can be intimidating, I work hard to demystify it. My promise to you is that if investing is foreign to you today, I do my best in the book to make it become familiar very quickly. You will find that once you get just a little bit of investing experience, you'll discover how simple it really is.

E = "Exponentiality"

The holy grail of investing is to achieve infinite returns. An infinite return means that you have zero of your own money in an investment that is still providing you with income. This book will show you how to find and build infinite returns and watch your wealth explode exponentially.

R = "Review, Rework, Repeat & Reward"

As with all things in life that we want to excel at, we need to be constantly assessing our processes and making adjustments. The life of an investor is no different. Then, once we have achieved a certain level of success, it's also just as important that we start to reap the harvest and enjoy the rewards of holding wealth.

To inspire you to dig in and get going, I want to encourage you to focus on possibly the most powerful wealth building tool in this book called, House Hacking. If you are willing to execute a house hack as it's designed, you could live in a beautiful house for FREE for the rest of your life (or until you have so much wealth that your house cost doesn't matter). The best part of house hacking is you can go from start to finish in 90 days or less. Then the savings from eliminating housing costs will enable you to start a powerful investment fund.

As you get inspired by the lifestyle hacks, I suggest you put them into action right away. Don't overanalyze and wait for the perfect time to start. Such a perfect time will never come. In fact, the more you wait the harder it will be to reach your goals. Also don't worry about doing it perfectly. Learning how to perfect each step is part of the process.

Grab a notebook, a highlighter and a comfy chair and prepare yourself to become a wealth building investor. I am so excited for you!

PART 1

THE AMERICAN DREAM

CHAPTER 1

WHAT IS THE AMERICAN DREAM?

ONLY IN AMERICA!

MRS. B

Warren Buffett, a man perpetually in the top five wealthiest people on the planet, loves to tell the American Dream story of Rose Blumkin. Rose was a Russian immigrant who arrived on a boat to America in 1917. She didn't speak a word of English and had never spent a single day of her life in school. She and her husband worked impossibly hard for fifteen years to save up a whopping $2,500. They invested that money to start a furniture store in their new hometown of Omaha, Nebraska.

Rose and her husband worked tirelessly for forty years in a very hostile environment. Rose's instinct was to buy furniture at wholesale prices and sell to the public at a price only slightly higher than her cost. She was playing the volume game, but her personal frugality enabled her to charge significantly less than anyone else in town. The local furniture companies did everything they could to force Rose out of business. They pressured banks not to lend to her, they tried to force furniture manufacturers to stop selling to her, and they tarnished her reputation publicly. Yet, she persisted, against all odds, to grow the Nebraska Furniture Mart (NFM) into the largest furniture store in the United States at the time.

In 1983, "Mrs. B" sold 80% of her furniture company to Warren Buffett for $60,000,000. They signed a one-page agreement to seal the deal. Since Mrs. B still had not learned to read and write, she signed with a simple squiggle on her signature line. Rose stayed on as the manager of NFM until she was 103 years old and died the following year. Perhaps the most touching part of her story is that from the time she learned English until her last days, Mrs. B required her family to sing "God Bless America" at every family meal.

We can't help but be inspired by Rose's story of success against all odds. As Americans, we know our country started from impossible odds and rose to be the most prosperous nation in human history. We got here through heaps of sheer force of will, tons of extremely hard work, and a maverick streak bent on problem-solving. It's a very American thing to say, "If you want to see me accomplish something, tell me I can't do it." We can't help but be in awe of the promise found in America as in very few other places on earth at any point in history. The American Dream seems to offer something unique. It offers a higher level of prosperity only kings could have commanded even just a couple hundred years ago.

Rose Blumpkin's story IS the American Dream. If Rose, a person who had every possible disadvantage, could rise to such staggering wealth and success, so can you. I assume you're reading this book because you haven't yet accomplished the promise of the American Dream. If you're like I was about 25 years ago, rather than basking in the fruits of the American Dream, you're stuck in an American nightmare where you can't seem to get ahead no matter how hard you work. In order to wake up from the nightmare and begin to experience the Dream, we must first understand how the nightmare can happen even to people who have all the advantages of being American.

The very concept of the American Dream is very much a part of the culture of America. Every American has heard the term and has some understanding of its meaning. It certainly means different things to different people. Most people I've asked say the American Dream is this idea that—regardless of race, religion, creed, age, gender, or education—every American, with enough hard work and determination, can be successful in life, financially and otherwise. Does that line up with what you know the American Dream to be?

I spent sixteen years living in five different countries outside the United States. One of the biggest surprises of living abroad is the perception non-Americans have of the United States. One of the first questions I was always asked by non-Americans was, "Does every American carry a gun?" We have Hollywood to thank for that one. My answer was, "No…unless you're from Texas."

At some point in the relationship with my foreign friends, the taboo issue of money inevitably came up. Most assumed all Americans were rich. Every non-American has heard stories, some true, some exaggerated, about the land of milk and honey that is the United States of America. While I made it a personal policy not to discuss money issues with my international friends, I quickly became aware that everyone on earth has an understanding of the "American Dream."

My friends in Guatemala would longingly talk about someday going to the United States to get work. They would tell me about "mojados," (wet) relatives, who were already there. It took me several weeks to realize that when a Guatemalan was "wet" in the U.S., that meant they got there illegally, entering the Rio Grande River on the Mexico side and crawling out wet on the U.S. side.

I am fully aware that the issue of illegal immigration is a hot-button topic for many Americans. Let me be clear that I am not making a political statement about immigration, legal or otherwise. I am simply illustrating how powerful of a concept the American Dream is. The idea of the American Dream is so powerful that good people are willing to risk their lives, pay unbelievable amounts of money, knowingly break laws, and leave behind everything they know—including their children, spouses, and parents—just for a chance to participate in the American Dream.

PAX ROMANA

The American Dream just might be the modern version of Pax Romana. During much of the ancient Roman Empire, there existed this idea that Roman citizenship granted its holders a peaceful life not attainable outside its borders. The sheer dominance of the Roman army and the power of the Roman economy was enough to create the perception that life inside the Empire was superior to life outside it.

For much of the Empire's existence, Roman citizens could go about raising their families, harvesting their crops, or hawking their wares in the market. They could buy Chinese silk, African wheat, Indian pottery, and Persian fabric. They could be entertained at free gladiator games and monthly chariot races.

Romans could freely travel from one end of the Empire to another, spanning 3,000 miles across all three known continents, with one passport and one currency, all under the protection of the legions. This life was in stark contrast to the life suffered among the "barbarians" outside the Empire, where the struggle to just survive dominated daily existence. The promise of Pax Romana is the primary reason why Rome was able to expand to rule almost 30% of the world's population for 500 years.

The United States of America has created a democratic republic, modeled partially after Rome, that has set it atop the world's modern economies with the world's standard currency, and by far the world's most powerful military. Like in ancient Rome, this combination has created the impression that living inside of America's borders is superior to living outside them.

America has evolved into a new kind of Roman Empire that not only promises a peaceful existence, but an historically prosperous one as well. Ancient Romans had Pax Romana. You, me, and Rose Blumpkin have the American Dream.

Many Americans feel like they are working really hard and are genuinely determined to succeed and build an American Dream. But the Dream is eluding us. While we still have faith in ourselves and hope for our ship to come in, we're beginning to wonder if the American Dream is not going to happen for us.

CHAPTER 2

THE AMERICAN DREAM NIGHTMARE

HARD WORK, DETERMINATION AND SUCCESS ARE NOT ALWAYS BEDFELLOWS.

Have you ever gotten up in the morning with an overwhelming dread of going to work? Have you ever been on your way to work tempted to just miss the exit and keep driving—scheming to go anywhere BUT your workplace? Have you ever been in a meeting with your incompetent boss where it took every ounce of your self-control not to quit right there on the spot? Perhaps you only held back because you feared being unemployed and having no income?

Have you ever put off paying bills because you knew you didn't have enough in the account to get every bill paid off, let alone have anything left over to enjoy life a little? Have you ever intentionally ignored your credit card balances for months on end because you know they are higher, maybe a lot higher, than you had ever feared they could be?

Have you ever felt anxiety about not having enough money for your retirement years when you don't have the strength to work like you can now and thought to yourself, "Is this all there is for me?" How often are one or more of these feelings and thoughts rolling through your mind? Several times a year…a month…a week? I certainly have. At my lowest point, I was feeling many of those things nearly every day.

The vast majority of Americans can relate far more to this hopeless feeling than to anything close to Rose Blumpkin's American Dream story. The American Dream for us can be more like a nightmare. We may work just as hard as her. We may be just as smart as her. We may even be just as gifted of a leader as she was. We are almost certainly more educated than her. However, we are stuck in a situation where breaking out to a high level of wealth and freedom, regardless of effort, intelligence, and education, seems almost impossibly out of reach.

If hard work, creativity, and determination are enough to achieve Rose Blumpkin's level of success, then why aren't we all living that experience, or at least seeing it develop on the horizon? The answer to that question has a lot of answers. However, I am going to argue that the single most fundamental reason why we struggle to break out of this hopelessness and achieve real success lies in our culture.

When I say culture, I am not only referring to culture in the societal sense that most of us would immediately think of. I'm referring to regional culture dictated by geography and climate. I'm talking about city cultures dictated by the industries where our jobs come from and even our sports teams. I am referring to our neighborhood cultures and extended and nuclear family cultures. Every single human being is a product of all of those cultures at the same time. There is no escaping this reality.

I have had the privilege to live in massive cosmopolitan cities like Buenos Aires, Argentina, which has a population of over fifteen million people who act and look European. I have lived in cool climate, high mountain towns like Quito, Ecuador, where my house sat at 10,000 feet above sea level, and the people were both sophisticated and rugged. I have lived in hot, tropical coastal cities like Rio de Janeiro, Brazil, where everyone is boisterous and colorful. I grew up in an agricultural town of 9,000 people in rural Idaho, surrounded by mountains, lakes, streams, and ski resorts where the pace of life was slower. Now I live in Phoenix, Arizona, a huge city surrounded by sand, cacti, and Native American reservations, where most of the population seems to be from somewhere else, bringing with them a myriad of identities.

After experiencing such a diverse array of cultures, I have discovered an unmistakable truth. Culture molds our worldview and thoughts in a more powerful way than ANY OTHER FORCE ON EARTH. Interestingly, most of us are only vaguely aware of the cultural force that works on us. Since our worldview and thoughts drive our actions, and our actions determine our results, our culture has a direct correlation to every eventual outcome of our lives.

You might be saying, "Well, fantastic…if culture drives my behavior and my behavior drives my actions and my actions determine my results, then I'm stuck because I can't change the culture from which I came." You're not entirely wrong, but you're also not entirely right.

As human beings, we are unbelievably resilient, creative, and able to use the power of our frontal cortex (the logical brain) in ways that other animals are simply incapable of. Let me try to imprint something profound on your mind. Rather than fight like mad to bend our outcomes to a different result than what our culture supports, why not fight like mad to bend our culture first, then let our actions and results change by default?

When I say we need to change culture, I am not referring to macro-culture, which for our discussion here could be defined as continental, national, regional, or even city-level culture. It is a rare Julius Caesar or Abraham Lincoln who is able to significantly bend macro-culture. What I am saying is that we can bend our micro-culture, which we can define as our neighborhood, our workplace, the family from which we came, and the nuclear family we may be forming now. Macro-culture changes extremely slowly and usually through dramatic events like Pearl Harbor, 9/11, and Covid-19.

Micro-culture, however, can be influenced and changed because we decide to change it. We can move to a new neighborhood pretty easily. We can find a new job, and we certainly can huddle the family together and build a new family culture. We don't need anyone's permission to do these things but our own.

If you are doubting your ability to change your micro-culture, spend a couple of minutes thinking about something Henry Ford said: "Whether you think you can or you think you can't, you're right." Changing micro-culture is indeed a hard thing to do because it is so deeply ingrained in our psyche. Changing our brains requires real intentional work to create new neural pathways that enable us to think in new ways and accept new worldviews. The key to being successful with this is deciding that it CAN be done.

WHY THE AMERICAN DREAM IS SO HARD TO REALIZE

Our modern America has developed a standard of living that is among the highest in the world. So before we get too hard on ourselves or American culture, we must acknowledge that even the poorest Americans are wealthier than billions of the world's poorest. That said, the American system has a voracious appetite for consumption, and that consumption is mostly paid for with debt.

The American system has grown more and more reliant on debt in the last 100 years. Politicians have discovered that the more money we borrow, the more money gets spent, which generates more taxes, which gives them more money to spend and grows the economy, which gets them reelected. So the entire system is reliant on everyone spending as much as possible, which requires borrowing as much as possible, regardless of how much risk that adds to individual families and even the country as a whole. This system is deeply ingrained, and we start to learn it in kindergarten.

At the beginning of the 20th century, most schools were small, and multiple grades were taught by one teacher in one room. Education was not very formal, and in many cases, children were not expected to go any further than eighth grade. All four of my grandparents finished eighth grade and then went to work. America was still largely agrarian, and the family farm required all hands on deck to keep the family afloat.

After World War II, everything changed. The Industrial Revolution had firmly taken hold, and the industrialized countries had seen farmers move in droves to the cities to work in factories. In the factory, a foreman barks out orders while standing over neatly organized rows of workers, each with a lunch pail stashed in a cubby with the worker's name on it. As the factories were shipped off to China and Mexico and industrial jobs gave way to office work, we continued the familiar structure. Now the office manager walks around with a clipboard amidst neatly organized rows of cubicles filled with workers who each have their lunch in a Tupperware with their name on it in the break room.

Considering this, it should be no surprise how our schools are organized. An authoritarian teacher stands at the front of a class full of students seated in desks neatly organized in rows with a lunch pail in a cubby with the student's name on it. Schools spend thirteen years teaching kids to assimilate into the factory or office worker mold. They spend almost no time or energy on helping kids understand Mrs. B's version of the American Dream.

In an attempt to be part of macro-cultural change, I started researching organizations that teach financial literacy and entrepreneurialism to children. The most prominent such organization I found was Junior Achievement. I read about their mock stock market training, among other things, and I got excited. I was impressed enough that I signed up to be an adult sponsor at their BizTown day that my eleven-year-old daughter was participating in through her fifth-grade class.

The day before BizTown, I gleefully thought to myself, "Finally, a way to help kids learn about how to develop real wealth and not just be cogs in the consumer machine—even if it is just one day out of the year." Six hours later, not only were my feet burning from the flurry of "on-my-feet-all-day" work keeping up with dozens of fifth graders, but I was also thoroughly disappointed in the entire premise of "BizTown."

Each kid applied for and interviewed for a job in one of several "businesses." Some were CEOs, some were CFOs, some were doctors, and some were technicians of varying kinds. None were board members, investors, inventors, or entrepreneurs. The worst part of the whole thing was that each business had the singular goal of getting a loan and working as hard as they could to pay off the loan by the end of the day.

Each kid had accounting tasks, mail delivery tasks, patient check-in tasks, etc. If they did their job well, they earned a paycheck that they could then use at the end of the day to spend on candy and toys.... Nobody got profit sharing, rent checks, dividends, or royalties. They might as well have all been wearing factory uniforms with a lunch pail in their cubbies! Even "BizTown" is conforming our kids to spin the economic hamster wheel to repeat the work, borrow, spend cycle. This is the death spiral that is the American nightmare.

We are told we have to go to high school. Once we get done with high school, we're told we have to go to college. College is so expensive, we are told we have to get school loans. Once we get out of college, we are told we now have to pay back the school loans. In order to do that, we have to get a job. So we get a job to pay off our school loans. Then we start a family and decide to buy a house.

The only way to get a house is to strap on the biggest loan yet. As life progresses, we get restless. We're working ridiculous hours to service our school and house debt. We've grown accustomed to carrying massive debt. So to address our restlessness, we buy expensive cars with long-term car loans and finance fancy vacations using our credit cards.

That's when we find ourselves stuck in the American nightmare. We barely make enough money to pay all of the monthly obligations we've agreed to, and the slightest financial storm can blow the whole thing down. We know it, and we stress about it constantly, but we don't know how to get out of it. Our problem is not an income problem. It's a consumption-through-debt problem. To gain control of the debt-driven consumption problem, let's get a firm grip on the two main forms of debt holding us back from building wealth: mortgage and credit card debt.

The Explosion of Home Mortgage Debt

Have you ever heard someone complain about how expensive housing is nowadays? The shocking truth is that the average cost of building a house today is nearly the same as the per-foot cost of building a house in 1950, adjusted for inflation. The problem is that the average square footage of homes today (2,467 sq. ft.), is almost three times larger than in 1950 (983 sq. ft.). Not only are our houses larger, but our family sizes have shrunk and are still getting smaller! According to the U.S. Census Bureau, the average family size went from 3.51 in 1950 to 2.61 in 2019. That means that each American's share of their house in 1950 was 280 square feet and today has more than tripled to almost the size of our 1950 home to 945 square feet! Before you blame the greedy consumer for wanting a larger house, we must ask ourselves why our houses have exploded in size.

In a word, debt is responsible for the mansionization of America. In the 1950s, most loans were amortized over a maximum of twenty years. Today, the standard home loan is thirty years. A longer payback schedule reduces the monthly payment, which enables us to borrow more to get a bigger house. Additionally, in the 1950s far fewer homeowners had a mortgage on their home at all.

According to morgagecalculator.com, between 1949 and the turn of the 21st century, [the] mortgage debt to income ratio rose from 20 to 73 percent! As our culture got more comfortable with home loans, we piled on even more debt. If that's not enough, the new trend in America is for both the husband and wife to work full-time jobs. Dual-income households are generally able to qualify for a higher mortgage payment, so we just keep buying larger and larger homes, all supported almost entirely by more debt.

Credit Card and Consumer Debt

The first widely adopted credit card, the Diners Club charge card, was invented and launched in 1950 by Frank McNamara. That single invention, and the credit card industry to follow, has done more to saddle people with high-interest, unsecured debt than any other financial instrument in known history. According to shiftprocessing.com, a full 44% of Americans carry an interest-bearing credit card balance every month. They also report that people who buy using a credit card spend up to 83% more than people paying with cash!

Studies have shown that human beings don't exhibit the same inhibition when spending with a credit card because they hand the clerk a piece of plastic for a few seconds only to receive that same piece of plastic back fully intact. The emotional weight of handing over a $100 bill and getting back a few dollars change is far more significant to our risk-reward brain.

In a typical year, the American consumer is credited with about 70% of total economic activity. In other words, no other sector of the economy comes even close to the importance of your average everyday American spending money on everything from houses and cars to dining out and buying groceries. This level of spending is not possible without many of us piling on tons of debt. The American system not only continues to turn a blind eye to the crushing debt its workers face, it has built an education system that guarantees it will continue.

We're going to dive into the HACKER method of wealth building that will teach you how to create a level of wealth that will not only enable you to live a life free from the borrow-spend-work cycle, but will create generational wealth. But before we dive deep into the how-to of building wealth, we need to finish the job of adjusting our micro-culture and getting our own identities oriented to building wealth. The next chapter will attempt to do just that. Get some coffee and find a quiet place to do some important foundational work.

CHAPTER 3

REBIRTH AS AN INVESTOR

TRY NOT! DO OR DO NOT. THERE IS NO TRY.

THE DAY I BECAME AN INVESTOR

It's the summer of 1993. I'm going into my junior year in high school. My family and I are on a road trip to visit my dad's family in Salem, Oregon. No offense to my cousins, aunts, uncles, and grandparents, but I remember almost nothing from that trip at all. I obviously had more important things on my sixteen-year-old mind. However, something happened at the tail end of that trip that I vividly remember that forever altered my life. It was so transformative for me that I can still picture myself sitting on the floor as I became aware of a conversation between my dad and his dad, my grandpa Tibbs.

They were talking about something that sounded very strange to me. They were considering buying a building that had two houses connected together. A duplex, they called it. At first, I just thought they were crazy. But as I tuned my ear more and more to their conversation, they seemed quite serious. They talked about how much money they would each have to put as a down payment and how they would handle collecting rent and paying the loan. The more they talked, the more I heard these ridiculous numbers like $100,000 to purchase it, $5,000 to fix it up, $25,000 for the down payment, $1,000 every month for the loan payment, etc.

I wasn't about to speak up, and I made sure they couldn't tell I was listening. The longer they talked, the more I thought they were nuts! I kept telling myself, "They are adults… surely they will come to their senses." Why would they risk so much money and deal with so much hassle just to provide a house to total strangers? I mean, they'd be on the hook to pay the house loan on a house they didn't even live in! They discussed clogged toilets, leaky roofs, water bills, and air conditioner replacements. They talked about the tenants destroying the building and even the possibility that it could burn down!

When I heard my dad say, "Let's call the agent and make an offer to buy it" I had to step in! "Dad! Are you crazy? You want to buy two houses, put complete strangers in them, and pay the mortgage every month? What would compel you to do such a dumb thing?" My grandpa and dad stopped in their tracks, just becoming aware that I was listening. They looked down at me, still sitting on the floor, and started chuckling.

Why were they laughing? I expected their reaction to be that of gratitude for saving them from such an expensive mistake. On the contrary, I could see in their eyes a sense of accomplishment at my question. They had successfully gotten a self-absorbed, single-minded teenager to engage with them in a life-lesson discussion. Their focus immediately shifted from the seriousness of a business deal to that of a noble challenge. They seized the opportunity to help me learn how to build wealth through real estate investing.

My grandpa had owned a few rental houses in decades past, but neither of them owned any at that time, so I'd never heard about anything like this before. The idea seemed so foreign to me. For over an hour, Grandpa and Dad walked me through the basics of buy-and-hold real estate investing. Obviously, I don't have a transcript of the conversation, but because this conversation had such a profound impact on the trajectory of my life, I do clearly remember the themes of the discussion. The conversation went something like this:

Me: Why would you want to put your neck on the line to have a stranger move into a house you are responsible for?

Grandpa: Because they will pay us rent in exchange for the right to live in the house.

Me: Yeah, but what if you get someone who won't pay the rent?

Dad: That's possible, but we will do our best to pick good tenants with a track record of paying rent on time.

Me: But what if they lose their job and can't pay you? You still have to pay the bank loan, right?

Grandpa: Yes, but if they don't pay, there are laws that allow us to make them move out so we can put someone else in who will pay.

Me: Okay, what about those weeks in between? Won't you lose money?

Grandpa: We have built in some lost rent from "vacancy" into our projections. So while we don't want it to happen, we're prepared for when it does.

Me: Okay, fine, but what about all of that interest? Every single month, you'll be paying hundreds of dollars in interest on the loan, right?

Dad: We won't pay the interest.

Me: Then the bank will take the house away, right?!

Dad: No, our tenants will pay the interest when they pay us rent. We're just the middleman transferring the rent over to the bank for the loan payment.

Me: That seems so risky. Why don't you just pay the full $100,000 so you don't have to pay all that interest? I mean, how would you sleep at night relying on perfect strangers to enable you to pay your bills?

Grandpa: We don't have $100,000. But even if we did, we'd rather not take that much risk!

Me: Risk?! A loan in your name isn't risky?

Dad: There is some risk, yes. But by taking out a loan, the bank is sharing the risk with us.

Me: That seems insane! I don't understand! How much money will you make after you pay the mortgage?

Grandpa: About $50.

Me: A day?

Grandpa: No, we'll make about $50 a month on average…

Me: [with an even more confused, frustrated look on my face] $50!? Why would you…?

Dad: $50 doesn't sound like much, but that's after paying all of the other expenses, factoring in future major repairs, a certain amount of lost months of rent for when tenants move out or get kicked out, and other things that come up.

Me: Is $50 a month enough for you to deal with the headache of unclogging toilets at 11 p.m.?

Grandpa: [fighting off laughter] *We were hoping you'd unclog the toilets!*

Me: *Yeah, right!*

Grandpa: [chuckling] *We will never unclog a toilet. We will pay a property manager to do that for us, and that's factored into the $50 profit.*

I began to soften just a bit; not because I agreed with the risky idea, but because they seemed to have a thought-out answer to all of my objections. The conversation resumed:

Me: *Still, aren't there easier and less risky ways to get $50?*

Grandpa: [graciously nodding as if to acknowledge the legitimacy of my question] *Well, it doesn't sound like much, but there are lots of other factors that make this work long-term. $50 a month isn't going to change our lives at all in the short term. But over several years or decades, the effect is huge. First, the tenants are paying all of the bills and putting $50 in our pockets. Included in those bills is the mortgage payment, which includes interest, but also includes the principal payment.*

Me: *I don't understand.*

Dad: *Every time you make a loan payment, you pay some interest and some of the loan balance. So the tenant is paying us rent, which we use to pay down the loan balance by about $75 every month. Not only are we getting $50 profit in our pockets, but our loan balance is reducing by an additional $75 every month. Again, we're just the middleman passing the tenants' rent over to the bank to pay the loan. It's not our money that pays the loan. Therefore, our net gain is actually $125 per month.*

Me: *But how long do you have to pay the mortgage payment?*

Grandpa: *Thirty years.*

Me: *What!?*

Grandpa: The longer the loan, the better to reduce our monthly out-of-pocket expense.

Me: What if the economy crashes and rents go down?

Dad: Look, there are risks. Anything can happen. But it's far more likely that rents will go up over time, not down. If you look at the long-term history of the United States, when have you ever heard of rents going down? They always eventually go up. So, while a $50 profit isn't much now, imagine if rents go up by an average of $25 a year for ten years. We will have two units, so that's $50 MORE profit each month every year. Ten years from now, rents could be $500 higher than they are now. And the best thing is, the mortgage payment won't change because it's on a fixed payment amount. So the $50 profit now, plus $75 in debt reduction plus increased rents, is gaining us roughly $650 every month by year ten. And we didn't unclog a single toilet!

Me: Okay… [still dubious but at least listening]

Grandpa: And then you have tax benefits too that reduce our tax bill to the government. That's worth a few hundred dollars every year on top.

Me: But you still have to pay all that interest! How much interest would you pay in thirty years?

Dad: A lot! It's like double the amount of principal!

Me: Exactly! See—I told you this was insane!

Grandpa: [holding onto patience by a thread or two] Brian, we don't have the money to buy the building outright. But even if we did, we'd still rather get a loan. We want the bank to take on some of the risk with us. In a way, the bank is a partner with us in this deal. They will make sure we have enough reserves, and they will have an incentive for us to be successful so that they are paid back. As long as our projections are correct, there will always be enough rental income to pay the mortgage, including interest.

Dad: Brian, you aren't understanding the idea of measured risk. Is there risk? Yes. Could we lose money? Yes. Could we even lose the building and the $25,000 down payment? Yes. However, your grandpa has done this before, and he knows how to calculate the risks. We have built a budget that is estimating lower than likely rents and higher than likely expenses, and it still pencils out.

Me: Pencils out?

Dad: Shows a profit at the end of the day that is attractive enough for us to take the risk.

Grandpa: There's a risk we'll get in a car wreck on the way to the office every day, but we get in the car anyway because the risk is necessary in order to get a paycheck. If we don't show up, we don't get paid. It's similar to this project. There's a small risk that things will go wrong, but to get the big payday at the end, we need to take on the small risk up-front.

Me: Okay, I think I understand why you are doing this. I still am nervous about how much money we are talking about. If it doesn't work like you think, it could be really bad.

Dad: You're right! We're nervous too. That's why we've spent four hours talking through the details. We want to make sure that we are measuring the risk correctly to be sure it's still a good deal long term.

I was quite surprised to learn that my dad and grandpa were nervous. I was shocked in a good way. I saw two grown men staring fear in the face and pushing forward in spite of it. It inspired me. Through their courage, something clicked for me. At the beginning of that conversation, I was convinced they were clumsily diving into a risky disaster. But I was now starting to see two capable, wise adults who were setting out to build wealth even when surrounded by uncertainty. $50 a month just isn't that much money. Even $650 a month isn't something to get too excited about. But if it worked on one project, maybe we could have ten more projects just like it. That's serious money.

Grandpa: There's one more element to real estate investing that we haven't even touched on yet. Did you know that I paid $5,000 for my first house? That same house is now worth $70,000. In America, real estate has a very strong history of going up in value over time. There are times when values drop, but give it enough time, and history says it will eventually increase in value. We can't predict how much this duplex will go up in value each year, but given ten years, chances are it will rise. It might even rise as much or more than we paid as a down payment. Our projections are assuming it does. So let's say we sell it in the tenth year. We will have been collecting increasing profit every year, ten of thirty years of the loan is paid off, and we get an extra $25,000 in home value gain on top.

Dad and Grandpa were staring at me eagerly, waiting to see if they had won me over. Remember, I was sixteen and loath to ever admit an adult actually knew anything intelligent, and equally loath to admit that I was wrong. So I stubbornly held onto my furrowed brow for a few moments. I was processing everything I had heard. They had answered every single one of the objections I knew would bring them to their senses. In the end, I had to admit that they seemed to know what they were talking about. I no longer could deny that the project seemed interesting. I left the room to find a piece of paper. I asked them to help me add up the numbers:

Profit in pocket
$50 per month in profit in year 1
$650 profit in year 10
~$300 per month profit average over 10 years
$300 X 12 months X 10 years =
$36,000 Profit!

Reduced loan amount
Total Principal paid by year 10 = approximately 16%
$12,000 loan balance reduction

Property value increase
10 years at 2.5% gain per year = 25% gain =
$25,000 value increase

Total project profit
$73,000!

They were going to almost triple the original down payment of $25,000! Staring at the numbers on the paper…sitting on my grandpa's floor…at the tender age of sixteen…I became a real estate investor.

UNLEARN WHAT YOU HAVE LEARNED

If you're a Star Wars fan, you probably recognize the phrase "unlearn what you have learned" as coming from the swamp scene from The Empire Strikes Back. Luke Skywalker is being trained to be a Jedi by 900-year-old Master Yoda. Yoda is struggling with young Luke's stubborn, know-it-all inability to learn the contrarian ways of the force. He soberly looks Luke in the eyes and says, "You must unlearn what you have learned." Luke half-heartedly replies, "Alright, I'll give it a try…" Yoda harshly shouts back, "NO! Try not! Do or do not. There is no try." This is my favorite movie exchange of all time, and the concept guides my career as an investor.

When I was on my grandpa's floor, I was Luke, and my dad and grandfather were Yoda. That was decades ago. Let's now imagine I am Yoda and you're Luke. What I am going to teach you in the HACKER method will seem like the opposite of what our culture (likely including the people who love you the most) has taught you to do your whole life. The truth is, what you have learned up until now is likely what is actually holding you back from learning the ways of wealth building.

I used to view things like loans, interest, clogged toilets, late rent checks, and even the volatile stock market as bad and scary risks to avoid. Once I learned the ways of wealth building, I accepted those things as vital parts of how wealth is built that must be embraced and used as indispensable tools. Now, I can't wait to get new loans, pay more interest, have clogged toilets, receive late rent checks, and watch the stock market fall because I know those things are a path to lasting wealth and a path to realize the real American Dream.

The key to building the kind of wealth that creates true financial and career freedom requires you to change your micro-culture mindset. You need to convert from being a consumer to being an investor. Just like when Neil Armstrong stepped off the lunar lander onto the surface of the moon, you are going to make one small transition in terms of words (consumer to investor) but one giant leap in terms of outcomes (financially trapped to independently wealthy).

If you take just one thing from this entire book, take this: From this point forward, you must take on the identity of an investor. Every time you spend money, you will ask yourself, how much will this purchase pull me away from or draw me closer to my financial goals? Consumers will almost always purchase things that pull them away from wealth. Investors will almost always purchase things that draw them closer.

As you dive into the HACKER chapters to come, you are going to have to struggle with unlearning the wealth-destructive consumeristic ways your culture has taught you. You also cannot enter with an attitude of, "Alright, I'll give it a try..." Saying you'll "try" is essentially saying you're halfway expecting to fail. If you halfway "try" and fail, you'll say, "Hey, at least I tried!" Can you see the self-fulfilled prophecy of failure in that mentality? I encourage you to search yourself at a deep level and decide if you are truly committed to the hard work and discipline of building serious wealth. Because the only way for the HACKER method to be effective is to do it with full confidence and 100% buy-in. Do or do not. There is no try.

What is my HACKER method? Simply put, it is a proven way to build significant wealth regardless of your income. And it goes like this:

H - Hack Your Lifestyle

A - Allocation Budgeting

CK - Cash Is King Investing

E - Exponentiality

R - Review, Rework, Repeat, and Reward

With that said, I am going to show you the primary things that we and other successful families have done to reach the wealthy class. Your journey to building wealth doesn't have to look exactly the same. However, two things do need to be exactly the same. First, you need to get more strategic on how you spend your money; and second, you need to figure out a way to increase your income. To be specific, you need to reduce your living expenses to 50% of your income. I know that might sound radical and out of reach. It's not! I assure you that you'll start to see how as you dive into the HACKER method! Let's roll!

PART 2

THE
HACKER
METHOD

HACK YOUR LIFESTYLE

CHAPTER 4

IDENTIFY AS A MINIMALIST

FOR EVERYTHING ELSE, THERE'S MASTERCARD.

From this point forward, everything I am going to teach you is principles and action steps that I have learned somewhere in my twenty-five-year journey of building lasting wealth on a very meager salary. Sometimes my own family saw the things I was doing and thought I was crazy. They don't think that now.

THE POOREST AMERICANS MAKE MILLIONS

Just eleven days after the attacks on America on September 11, 2001, the U.S. Congress enacted legislation that created the "911 Fund." Seven billion dollars ($7,000,000,000) were appropriated to compensate the victims and their families from the tragedy of the attacks of September

11. Never before in American history had such a fund been created to compensate victims of this kind in this way.

I knew that no amount of money would soothe the pain of the lost family members, but I was fascinated by how the government went about deciding how much money to grant the families who had lost loved ones in the attack. Aside from a few other factors, the government essentially attempted to calculate the likely future earnings of the people who had died. They assessed their most recent income, looked at how many working years they likely had left, adjusted for pay increases, inflation, improved experience, and skills, and wrote checks.

Aside from the cold reality of the process, I remember being shocked at learning how much money typical Americans would earn in their lifetime. The average death compensation from the 911 Fund was $2,082,128! The highest amount was $8,600,000! Even the families of entry-level workers were getting seven-figure checks.

When I saw these numbers, I did some simple math to make sure I was understanding right. Here's what I found: If you consider someone entering the job force making $36,000 per year and earning pay raises equal to 3.8% (the average inflation over the last sixty-two years according to WorldData.info) every year and remaining in the job force for forty years, they will earn a total of $3,263,901 in salary. What?! If you enter the workforce making $55,000 per year, you'll earn almost $5,000,000! The first question I had after reading that was, "Why aren't all Americans millionaires!?" The second question I asked myself was, "Why do so many Americans die with little or nothing?" The answer to these questions is found in one word: "consumption."

MINIMALIST TO MILLIONAIRE

While consumption is a fact of life and unavoidable for anyone living in any modern society, the extreme level of consumption, or consumerism, is the culprit that robs its citizens of acquiring wealth. The problem of poverty in America and similar advanced economies is not income but consumption.

To address this issue and help you master the first step in the HACKER method, I want to introduce you to the concept of minimalism. Please understand that I do not care if you embrace the philosophy behind the minimalist movement or not. I merely want to introduce a lifestyle that is the antithesis of consumerism. The taming of hyper-consumerism tendencies is the key to building wealth, especially for those of us who do not earn large salaries.

There are two fundamentals of minimalism. First, minimalists are loath to own items they don't absolutely need. Second, minimalists are driven to declutter their lives by getting rid of physical things as a symbol of clearing their souls. For us, however, training ourselves to spend less on things we don't absolutely need will free up our expendable income to invest. Liquidating some of the things we already have will create an instant seed fund that can jump-start our investing career, which we discuss in the step titled, "Cash Is King Investing."

Serious minimalists have rules that ensure they live on less. Many only allow themselves to keep things they use daily or at least weekly. Others only allow themselves to purchase something new if they first get rid of something else they already have. Some go so far as to stop doing things they like to do because they need too many things in order to do them. Cooking is a good example. It's not uncommon for chefs, for example, to have hundreds of little gadgets and appliances, most of which they rarely, if ever, use.

I am not advocating going to the extreme here. Rather, I would suggest you set rules for new purchases and stick to things you really need to keep functioning at a high level until you have the wealth you need to return to purchasing comfort items that aren't necessary but are just nice to have.

If you are struggling with the concept of a minimalist lifestyle, let me illustrate to you why this is all-important. Let's say you decide to contribute $500 every month into your investing fund (I am actually going to show you how to invest much more in the Allocation Budgeting step), but over time you start cheating to buy that fourth pair of shoes, take that extra weekend getaway, or buy the latest big-screen TV that's a few inches larger than your current big-screen TV. By the end of the year, you're only depositing an average of $100 per month in your investing fund. If that trend continues over the course of twenty years, and if you were to grow your wealth at the same rate the stock market goes up each year, your spur-of-the-moment splurges would have cost you $265,726 in future wealth. Buying those shoes and TVs suddenly feels counterproductive.

Consumers build a lifestyle that puts pleasure and comfort first and foremost and, by default, puts building wealth last. If you have done even a little of this, don't feel bad. I've done it too, and you are probably surrounded by people who don't even realize they are forfeiting wealth for immediate gratification through the endless acquisition of stuff. Just think about the most popular corporate slogans. My favorite is, "There are some things money can't buy. For everything else, there's Mastercard."

Mastercard's message of unbridled consumption isn't even subtle! It's nearly impossible to earn an average wage and generate wealth when we spend our incomes on the stuff that Mastercard will help you buy even though you can't afford it. Instead, through the HACKER method, you will learn how to invest your money now so that in the future, you will be able to buy all of that stuff 100 times over if you wanted.

Your wealth will grow on a sliding scale that is 100% directly correlated to two factors. First, how much money can you put to work now to kick-start your investing career? Second, how much of your income can you commit to investing going forward? The more you consume, the less you can invest, and the harder it will be to grow significant wealth. The more you can invest now and the less you consume going forward, the faster and higher your wealth will multiply.

Take a look at these three investment scenarios to better understand the effect of beefing up your starting investment fund and reducing your consumption going forward:

1) If you can scrape together $10,000 to start and add another $1,000 every month to your investment fund for 30 years and earn 10% annual return:

Your Net Worth = $2,148,422

2) If you can invest $25,000 to start, invest $2,000 every month to your investment fund for 30 years and earn 10%:

Your Net Worth = $4,384,091

3) If you invest $50,000 to start, and add another $3,000 every month to your investment fund for 30 years and earn 10%:

Your Net Worth = $6,794,255

Go to www.TheUnexpectedInvestor.com/Calculators to plug your own numbers into my free future net worth calculator and dream about what is possible.

STAGE AN ESTATE SALE

You might be excited to start reaching toward those kinds of net worth numbers, but you don't have $50,000, $25,000, or even $10,000 lying around to create your investment seed money. While you may not have that much money lying around in cash, you might be surprised how much value you have in the stuff you've already accumulated. This is where I suggest you stage an estate sale. The purpose of the estate sale is to pay off high-interest debt, and anything left over will create that seed money fund to start investing.

If you are the guy or gal with a house or garage full of toys and late-model cars, you have a ton of money sunk into stuff that probably gets relatively little use or could be replaced with something far less expensive. Put that money to work now, be diligent and patient, and be a multi-millionaire on the other end.

To do an effective estate sale, you should model professional estate liquidators. Estate liquidation companies have perfected the art of generating tons of cash for their clients and net much more money than a typical garage sale, where everything sells for $1. First, they hold a three-day (Friday to Sunday) weekend "Estate" sale in the home with most stuff priced high to start, then lowered on the second and third days. They almost never negotiate posted prices until day three. Each item's price is firm on day one. On day two, everything but the biggest ticket items is 30% off the original price. On Sunday, they go to 50% off the original price. Any big-ticket items that are still unsold after day three get sold online for the best possible price on Facebook Marketplace or OfferUp, for example. The psychology of this strategy encourages people to pay the higher rate on Friday for fear that someone else will get it before they come back. By Sunday, very few items remain, and the cash haul is impressive.

Pick a date for your sale at least a couple of weeks in the future to give yourself enough time to price everything and advertise. Then create your big-ticket sale list. Identify everything you are willing to part with that will sell for over $100, including the really big items like boats, snowmobiles, and cars (but read the next chapter on hacking your transportation before deciding to sell your car). Then, a week before your estate sale, start advertising the sale by highlighting the big-ticket items on social media. No matter what, don't agree to sell those big items before the official sale because those items are driving traffic to your sale.

Two days before your sale, mark your neighborhood well so people can find you, and tell everyone you know to come check it out. Set out the things you will sell throughout your home, and watch the stuff you barely use turn into a wealth-building investing seed money fund! Now tell yourself, "I am staring at the seed money that is going to produce millions!"

One cautionary note before we proceed. There will be a point in this process of selling your stuff that you look at an item that truly should be sold, and your emotional brain is going to try to convince you to keep it. Then you will see another item, then another. You may look at the weight bench and decide to keep it because you think that you're magically going to start working out. My advice is to sell it and do bodyweight exercises instead. If you don't resist this temptation, pretty soon your investing seed money is seriously depleted, and your future wealth-building prospects with it.

I am reminded of an old movie with Steve Martin called The Jerk. In that movie, Steve's character earns millions from a clever invention. That invention eventually fails, and he loses everything. As he's walking away from his mansion, he yells, "I don't need any of this stuff!... except this ashtray. I need this ashtray." He then slowly walks through his luxurious office and keeps finding things he can't live without. By the time he exits the scene, his arms are full of the ashtray, a ping-pong paddle game, a TV remote control, a book of matches, a lamp, a magazine, and a single dining room chair. Resist the temptation to do as the jerk does and let the stuff go you know you don't need. If you haven't used it in the last two or three months, you probably don't need it.

As we close out this chapter, I am reminded of the spending habits of my teenage son. He loves gadgets and constantly discovers new gizmos he can't live without. He obsessively researches which company makes the best version of this gadget, then endlessly schemes ways to find the money to buy it. By the time he makes the order and it arrives on our doorstep, his enthusiasm is at a fever pitch. He rips open the box, assembles the gadget, and disappears for a couple of days, discovering all the uses of the gadget. On the third day, almost like clockwork, he loses his enthusiasm, stashes it in his closet, and emerges looking for the next gadget like a hungry shark searching for his next meal.

Just as I am trying to help my son learn to manage his insatiable appetite for gadgets, I want to challenge you to look at your spending behavior to see if you have any similar spending patterns. There's a reason why the minimalist mindset is the first step in wealth building. The fastest way to build wealth is to take control of your consumption habits. Remember, our problem is not an income problem. Our problem is primarily a consumption problem. Conversely, the solution is to use a portion of that money we used to spend on stuff toward building a multi-million dollar investment estate.

CHAPTER 5

HACK YOUR TRANSPORTATION

NOTHING WORTHWHILE IS EASILY OBTAINED.

Joey Chatterton barged into my freshman dorm room, proudly bragging that his "1970 Toyota Starlet just kicked over to zero miles." Apparently, he didn't get the response from the four of us he wanted. We were in the middle of an intense game of NBA Jam and didn't even acknowledge his presence. So Joey moved between us and the screen and repeated, "Hey, idiots! My car just rolled over to zero miles." My roommate Jason very calmly replied, "!*&^%* move before I gut you."

Jason was justifiably upset because he was playing Michael Jordan, and MJ was ON FIRE! Joey just stood there staring at us. "Out of the way, moron," we all yelled in unison. Joey stubbornly persisted. "You don't understand! I just drove past mile 999,999 on my Starlet, and the odometer started over at 000,000!" The four of us looked at each other, then looked at Joey. Then we lunged at him, picked him up, threw him on the couch, and resumed our game.

Despite our brutish frat boy response to his inconsiderate interruption of our JAM session, I remember being at least a little intrigued. I had never even considered the fact that some odometers have only six digits, and I had never heard of a car lasting enough miles for the digit count to matter.

In hindsight, as impressive as one million miles is for any car, that car was a huge net negative for Joey for a lot of reasons. The car was the ugliest and oldest car in our dorm parking lot, which was full of ugly, old cars. If Joey wanted to actually drive the Starlet somewhere, he had to spend a few minutes just getting the thing to start without flooding it. Then, he would sit in the car for at least ten minutes revving the engine so the car could warm up enough to actually drive without repeatedly dying on the road.

Joey was constantly complaining about the cost of fixing things on it. The piece of junk was too small and broken to haul us all around, so we almost never rode in it. Most importantly of all, it was NOT helping him with the ladies. So why did Joey love his car so much? Why did he keep it way, way past its useful life? I don't know the specific answers to those questions, but I know the answer has a foundation in emotion, not logic.

Before we point our collective fingers at Joey and laugh at his irrational attachment to his Starlet, maybe we should all go out to the driveway and take a hard look at what we drive and ask why. Why do you own your vehicle? Or vehicles? What emotional reasons drove you to buy the cars you did, and what are the rational or logical ones you use to justify it?

We've all heard that humans buy things emotionally and justify the purchase using logic. Americans, in particular, are known for their obsession with cars. So, it should come as no surprise that emotion is the primary driver of our car purchases.

Go pretty much anywhere else on earth, and the cars are much smaller, more boxy, more fuel efficient and…well…more boring—err, logical. The Dodge Ram 3500, sold in America, seats five passengers. It's a beautiful beast of a machine. It weighs over 6,000 pounds, is twenty-one feet long, eight feet wide, and six-and-one-half feet tall. It can move its five passengers at the cost of twelve miles to the gallon of gas.

Compare the Ram pickup to the most popular car in Europe, the Volkswagen Golf, which also seats five people. We can't describe the Golf as a beautiful beast of a machine with a straight face. The Golf weighs just 2,870 pounds (52% lighter), is fourteen feet long (33% smaller), five feet, ten inches wide (27% thinner), and just four feet, nine inches tall (27% shorter), and can move five people almost three times farther at a rate of thirty-four miles to the gallon.

I know the Dodge Ram has different utility over a passenger car like the Golf. However, as primary passenger vehicles, trucks are a uniquely American phenomenon. The Dodge Ram is a symbol of America, just as the Volkswagen Golf is a symbol of Europe.

To hack your way into the wealthy class, you most likely need to start looking at your vehicle situation in a new way that defies your culture's view on cars. First, it's vital for you to take a logical look at your current vehicle situation. Add up your monthly expenses related to all your vehicles for loans, insurance, gas, maintenance, and depreciation.

POP-UP DEFINITION

Depreciation - the loss in value of your asset over a period of time.

In almost all situations, cars lose value as they rack up miles and get older. Even though you don't write a check every month for your car's depreciation, you absolutely pay that depreciation expense each time you trade in your vehicle. Also, if you start looking at your life like a business (which wealth hackers do), your vehicles are a constant downward drag on your net worth because they are costing you money to operate and are losing value each and every month.

There are a lot of sites out there that can estimate your model's depreciation, but I like caredge.com. I also invite you to log on to www.TheUnexpectedInvestor.com/Calculators and use my free vehicle hacking calculator to make the process easier for you. The chart below is my stab at estimating the average vehicle cost for the average American household:

Cost Item	Monthly Cost Per Car	Annual Cost Per Car	2 Vehicles After 20 Years	Notes
Car Loan	$566.14	$6,794	$271,746	Original $30,000 loan, 5 year, 5% interest
Full Coverage Insurance	$125.00	$1,500	$60,000	
Gasoline	$180.00	$2,160	$86,400	$3.60/gallon, 24 MPG, 1,200 miles/month
Maintenance	$75.00	$900	$36,000	
Depreciation	$139.58	$1,675	$67,000	$30,000 purchased new and kept 4 years
Total	$1,085.72	$13,028.64	$521,145.76	

The chart above makes the following assumptions: 1) You will constantly hold two vehicles for the next twenty years. 2) You buy those vehicles new and hold them for an average of four years. 3) You will pay $33,000 and put 10% down with a five-year loan at 5% interest.

This scenario says driving yourself around town over the next twenty years will cost you over half a million bucks. Let's kick this up a notch and look at it from a more advanced finance view. Imagine you were able to eliminate your vehicle expense and instead invest that vehicle money at a 9.7% annual return (average stock market's performance over the last ninety years). You'd flip a $521,146 loss into over $721,000 in the bank. That's a $1.25 million swing in your favor!

We are emotional creatures, and we are not going to stop making decisions with our emotions. My goal here is that the emotion of converting a half-million-dollar loss into a massive potential gain creates an emotion more powerful than the emotion that drives you to make expensive and illogical vehicle purchases.

Some people buy cars to impress their friends. Some do so to appear to be wealthy and successful. Others do it to appear adventurous or to feel the rush and freedom of power and speed. Channel those same desires into wealth building with a long-term vision, and understand that having lower vehicle expenses now will be a wealth engine that will accelerate your ability to truly impress, actually become wealthy, experience real adventures, and feel that freedom and power in a much more authentic way.

THE LOGIC VEHICLES TO OWN

Now let's explore ways to reduce or even eliminate our vehicle expenses. If you are motivated enough, there's even a chance to flip your vehicle from a financial drain to an income producer. Let's first take a look at practical vehicle ownership. Aside from owning rare collector vehicles, there's no realistic way to own a vehicle that goes up in value over the long haul.

Our job now is to do the research to find the car that will lose the least value, cost the least to drive, have the least maintenance expense, and be reliable enough to get us from A to B. The right vehicle to satisfy these requirements may be very different from one person to the next. You may need a pickup for work. You may need six or seven seats to fit all your family members. Or you may just need one seat to get to and from work. It is up to you to factor in your needs as you calibrate your vehicle strategy to maximize your wealth-hacking journey.

In my research, I have found that the best age of car to buy is one that is around seven to nine years old. Cars that are newer than seven years old have a steeper depreciation rate than cars older than ten years. Also, insurance costs are tied closely to the replacement cost of the vehicle, so cheaper cars are cheaper to insure. Your maintenance costs will most likely be higher, but as my car lot-owning brother always says, "Vehicles are much more reliable now than they were even twenty-five years ago."

If you're tempted to get a car that is a lot older, I would encourage you to think twice. I made a costly mistake in my twenties when I purchased a 1987 Chevy Blazer for $800. The car was already twenty-two years old and not running the best. After I purchased it, I noticed that it was leaking oil. It wasn't just leaking a little...I had to put a quart of oil in it every week to keep the oil level full.

I must have forgotten to fill the engine with oil for a week or two because one day, the engine seized up and ground to a halt on the highway. The jarring feeling of an engine locking up as you're cruising along at fifty miles per hour is one I don't wish on anyone.

The worst part of my Blazer story is that the vehicle still haunts me to this day. Occasionally, when I am starting a new account online, an automated system searches the public records to authenticate my identity. Inevitably, the system pulls up four vehicles, three of which are random cars I have never owned, and one of which in the public record as a car I have held title to. Every single time, it's that stupid Blazer. I guess it's the internet's way of keeping me humble. I encourage vehicle frugality, but don't go cheap. There's a huge difference.

The bottom line is that the ratio of depreciation versus maintenance and insurance costs are mostly in your favor for cars at or around ten years of age. Much newer than that, and you'll lose too much in depreciation. Any older than that, and your maintenance expenses and time lost in the shop may exceed your depreciation savings. The next factor to consider is fuel economy. Think about making a purchase based on MPG instead of the 0-to-60 speed.

If you drive a fuel-efficient car that gets thirty-five miles to the gallon and you drive 13,000 miles each year and gas costs $3.60 per gallon, you'll spend $1,337 a year on gas. If your sports car or gigantic truck gets half that mileage, simply double your gas expense to $2,674 per year. Finally, the make and model of the car is important to an extent as well. My car dealer brother swears by Toyota, Nissan, Honda, and Mazda. He says these Japanese brands are the best built, get great mileage, cost the least to operate, and retain their value better than all the other mass-market cars.

Perhaps the most important part of owning vehicles is to do so without financing. Ever wonder why car salespeople love to sell you financed cars? There are three reasons, and they're all measured in dollars. Your dollars, to be specific.

First, they know they can sell you a more expensive car if they can leverage that thing to the heavens. We've all seen those studies that show consumers spend significantly more money using credit than when they pay with cash. Car dealers know this and use it to their advantage. Most sales commissions are on a percentage of the sale. So, the sales rep's primary incentive is to get you to spend as much as possible.

Second, if the dealership handles financing in-house, they generate interest on the loan balance for the life of the loan. Even if they don't finance in-house, they likely have a financial benefit when referring financing to their partner bank. Either way, the higher the loan amount, the higher their income.

Third, financing packages almost always include costly setup fees. Some of those fees go directly into the pocket of the sales guy who signed you up. Once again, the more you spend and finance, the more they make.

All three factors mean less money in your pocket and more in theirs. One time I was trading in my car, and throughout the whole ridiculous negotiation process, the sales guy kept talking as if I was going to finance the car I was buying.

I didn't correct the salesman because I knew he would be more flexible on the terms if he assumed he was getting financing kickbacks. He got visibly agitated when, right before signing, I said I was going to pay in cash. He tried to backpedal on the price we had agreed to by saying that price was an internet-only price, which was complete bologna.

If you have expensive cars on loans, my advice is to liquidate those cars, pay off the loans, and use the money left over (hopefully there's money left over) to buy a reliable seven-year-old car and get out of the most costly part of car ownership—the monthly loan payment.

Let's re-run the numbers on what your long-term vehicle expense will look like if you are able to restructure your transportation as we've discussed here. The chart below assumes you have no car loans, have reduced your insurance by 33%, increased your gas mileage by 11 MPG, doubled your maintenance expense, and reduced your depreciation rate to just 4% per year (versus the 20% suffered in a car's first year).

Cost Item	Monthly Cost Per Car	Annual Cost Per Car	2 Vehicles After 20 Years	Notes
Car Loan	$0.00	$0	$0	$0 loan - purchased with cash
Full Coverage Insurance	$82.50	$990	$39,600	Reduced 33%
Gasoline	$123.43	$1,481	$59,246	$3.60/gallon, 35 MPG, 1,200 miles/month
Maintenance	$150.00	$1,800	$72,000	Doubled
Depreciation	$50.00	$600	$24,000	$15,000 purchase price at 10 yrs old
Total	**$405.93**	**$4,871.14**	**$194,845.71**	

In this scenario, you've reduced your twenty-year vehicle costs by over $300,000!

In some situations, the smartest vehicle to own is not to own one at all. Now that you know your transportation costs, if you live in a large metro area with good public mass transit options, perhaps you should consider selling your vehicles completely and converting to public transport. Owning real estate in good neighborhoods where public transport is available can increase in value, and it may be a good solution to reduce your travel costs and turbocharge your wealth-building journey. For five of the last seventeen years, I did not own a vehicle and relied 100% on public transportation. Never having to remember where you parked your car, or worry about door dings and car repairs, is very easy to get used to.

To make vehicle ownership as easy as possible, I have created the LOGIC car ownership formula.

L - Lose the loans and leases

O - Over 35 MPG

G - Get in at 7 years, trade at 11

I - Insist on reliability and resale value

C - Convert your car into a business

The "C" in the LOGIC formula may not be for everyone. However, if you are really motivated to hack into the wealthy class, this next section could be helpful to you.

GENERATE CASH FROM YOUR RIDE

Along with purchasing a more practical vehicle, there are a few ways you can hack your transportation to generate cash. My warning here is to make sure you don't sacrifice too much time chasing small dollars when your time could be better used finding better returns on your time spent. Perhaps when you are first getting started, you can devote more time to the ideas in the next few pages. However, you should periodically reassess the time you're giving to this hack. Once your income and net worth have started to climb, there may be more productive ways to spend your time. With that said, let's explore the different ways a vehicle can generate income.

The lowest barrier to entry to generate cash from your vehicle is to become a gig worker driver. Apps like Uber and Lyft enable anyone with a license, a car, and the ability to follow a GPS to access quick cash. A word of caution, however. I almost always ask my Uber drivers if they're happy with the income and the work. Usually the answer is, "I'm just doing this temporarily to make extra cash," or "I lost my job and am doing this until I find something else." That answers my question. According to ridester.com, most drivers earn less than $15 per hour after factoring in fuel, depreciation, and maintenance costs. Maybe a way to squeeze cash out of your car would be only to drive in idle time when you have nothing else to do and are truly in a hustling mood.

Another option to generate some cash from your car is to list it on a person-to-person sharing site such as Turo. These sites enable vehicle owners to rent their cars to people needing a car for as little as one day. There are hassles and costs associated with lending your car out to strangers, so do your research before you jump in. However, once you get your car listed, you can set your calendar to make your vehicle available only when you know you don't need it.

Think for a minute about how much you use your vehicle and how much time it sits idle. Suppose you are a two-car family and your drivers have both Saturday and Sunday off from work. In that case, chances are you need only one vehicle on weekends anyway and can easily put one car to work on Turo without affecting your normal routine. When you go on vacation, you can also set your account to rent both your cars out while you're gone and rack up some income as you work on your tan at the beach.

Yet another way to hack your vehicle is to find someone to carpool with. Assuming you don't work at a large company that already has a pool of people living near you and working at your building, you may want to find a carpooling app like Moovit or a local carpooling website to find someone from your neighborhood who commutes to your area for work. Convenient carpool options may enable you to drop from two cars to one and just carpool with others permanently.

One final hack most people have never considered. Assuming you've decided to reduce down to one vehicle, you successfully decluttered your garage in the minimalist mindset phase, and you find yourself with at least one empty garage bay, consider renting out your garage spot for $50-$100 per month. Likely people are living near you who have run out of space and are willing to pay you rent for yours. If you decide to explore this, factor in the cost to install a digital garage door opener, and put a deadbolt on the door to your house from your garage to increase security.

Another vehicle hack for those of us who are extra motivated to accelerate wealth building and are shameless about it: Sign an advertising deal with a local business, and let them wrap your car or mount a sign on the roof with their marketing messaging. Several companies out there will pay you hundreds of dollars to drive around with their branding on your vehicle. While this option may cramp the style of many, it is an additional option to accelerate your path to building wealth. Check out Wrapify, Free Car Media, Sticker Ride, Carvertise, Nickelytics, and Pay Me For Driving to see if any of these companies market in your area.

Assuming you trade in your cars with loans on them for the older, more economical cars, and assuming your monthly expense per vehicle is $405 per month as I have speculated in the chart on page 55, let's calculate what it will take to cover that $405 cost through these income-generating ideas.

If you decide to join Uber and can make $15 per hour above all expenses, you'd only need to drive about twenty-seven hours to cover your transportation costs for the month. That's two Saturdays and a Sunday at eight hours each. If you could rent your car for $60 per day on Turo, you'd need to rent it out for seven days a month. If you found three workmates that were willing to carpool with you to work, you could charge them just $6 per day each and cover your costs.

I have very fond memories of my college mate Joey. I even appreciate the comical memories of his Starlet. But Joey's goal to pay and do whatever it took to drive that junker over one million miles was just not a good use of his money, time, or energy. The primary reason I shared the Starlet story with you is because I assume you easily see the folly of the emotional decision to own and operate that car. Now, I want you to look critically at your own emotion-driven car purchasing decisions and realize that buying a new, sparkly car with debt is actually more detrimental to your wealth-building journey than what Joey did with the Starlet.

Whenever I go to purchase a vehicle, I think equally about Joey's Starlet and the guy driving a Dodge Viper. This helps me steer clear of an emotional car-buying mentality. Am I using my resources in a way that considers the long-term financial vision for my life? Or am I chasing emotionally charged goals that are superficial and, more importantly, hurting my long-term success?

Take action today to hack your transportation. Whether your car has 1,000,000 miles or costs $80,000, it doesn't impress your neighbor for very long. Your vehicles may be quick and powerful, but they don't make you quick and powerful. Overly expensive cars are one of the primary things holding you back from your true financial potential. Make the commitment today to liquidate your emotional cars and buy with LOGIC.

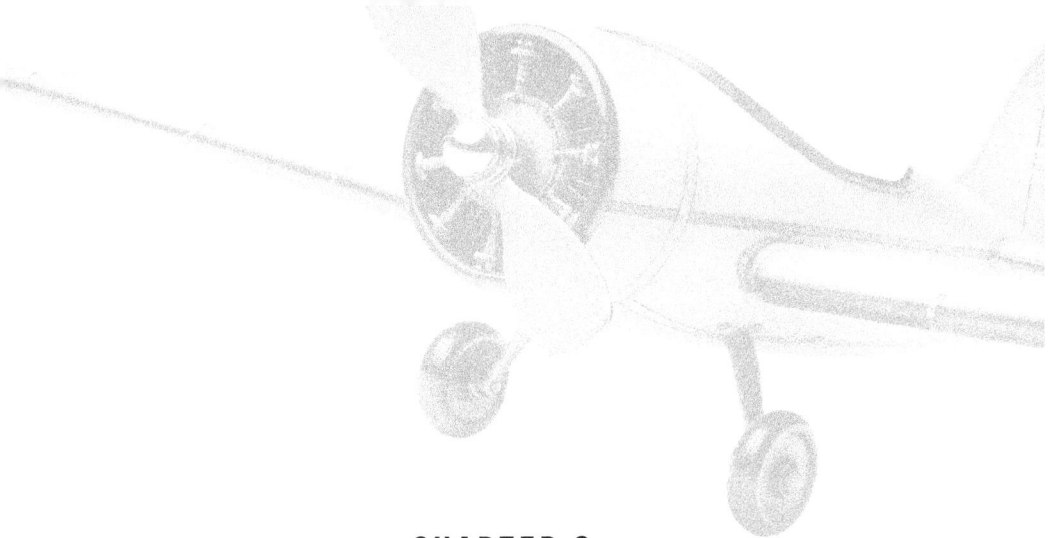

CHAPTER 6

HOBBY HACKS & SIDE HUSTLES

DESTINY IS NOT PREDETERMINED: IT'S A BLANK CANVAS AWAITING YOUR ARTISTIC TOUCH.

TRADE YOUR EXPENSIVE HOBBIES FOR LUCRATIVE SIDE HUSTLES

Human beings are dynamic creatures. What sets us apart from the rest of the animal kingdom is our high intelligence and ability to adapt to our environment and circumstances through innovation. Our ancestors spent all their time figuring out how to build tools to be better hunters, how to cultivate crops to reduce food gathering time, and how to create better shelters, clothing, etc. We have made so much progress through innovation that we no longer have to spend all of our time merely surviving.

Now, we have machines that do almost everything our ancestors did by hand. All but those living in extreme poverty have electric lights, pressurized water, dishwashers, clothes washers, and microwaves. Instead of hunting for our food, we make our Walmart grocery order on our phone while we sit on the couch in our underwear watching Netflix. A few hours later, our order arrives at our doorstep, and we are annoyed that we have to walk them into the house and put them in the fridge. Even that step can be eliminated by signing up for Walmart+. They'll walk into your house and put your food away for you. Contrast that to our ancient ancestors who killed their neighbors to steal their food....

The automated life has created the relatively new phenomenon of spare time. Spare time is not always a good thing for highly intelligent creatures. We need stimulation and a challenge. Thus, hobbies have become a standard method by which human beings use up their spare time. Most hobbies are a good thing. They engage our intelligence and ingenuity and reduce our stress levels. Hobbies can be a healthy distraction from the stressful time we spend making a living.

However, in our consumer-driven culture, hobbies can sometimes be very expensive and, therefore, destructive to wealth building. I have some friends who love to fish and waterski. They have a $50,000 boat and all the boat gear you could imagine. They have more boogie boards, water skis, wakeboards, float tubes, fishing rods, coolers with waterproof speakers built in, and other accessories than I can count. They hook up their $50,000 boat, holding $10,000 of gear, to their $50,000 SUV, which they upgraded so they could tow the boat, and away to the lake they go.

Every weekend between June and August, they are on the water. Sometimes they come home with a stringer full of fish and talk about how much people spend at the grocery store for fish this good. I think sometimes we try to find small victories amidst our consumer-driven choices in an attempt to justify our luxury-level spending. But we all know deep down that even if we catch 1,000 fish from our $110,000 investment, we're never going to break even from the money saved on our grocery budget.

I am not going to tell you to stop having hobbies. I am going to encourage you to stop doing hobbies that cost you money, and trade them in for a hobby or two that can generate money for you. There are infinite ways you can make money through a hobby. There are some who will warn you that monetizing your hobby will kill your passion for it. I concede this is possible. However, the best way to hack your way into the wealthy class is to reduce your living expenses, and hacking your hobbies into income-generating side hustles is a very effective way to accelerate your wealth. If you find yourself losing your passion for a hobby due to the monetization aspect, change hobbies or give yourself an exit strategy. Remember, as your wealth grows, you will reassess your lifestyle hacks and adjust as needed. You shouldn't have to do side hustles once your investments start to generate strong returns.

If you love to tinker and build stuff, maybe try building custom furniture or hire yourself out to be a handyman or handywoman. If you don't want to deal with customers face to face, you could get good at building one thing to sell on eBay or to a local furniture store. If you love to barbecue, keep your grill and become a barbecue caterer. If you love to cook, keep your expensive knife set, and put yourself out there to be a chef for hire. My brother hired a private chef for $300 to come to my house to cook dinner for my wife, mom, and sister-in-law. He was in our home for all of sixty minutes. That's decent cash for anyone.

Now, about that $50,000 boat sitting at the RV storage place...I'm cracking open the door for you to keep it too. Let me tell you a story about my brother-in-law, Steven Bramhall. He is a fishing NUT. I implore you to find someone who knows more or cares more about fishing than Steven. He has forgotten more about fishing than I ever knew. He was one of those guys with a $50,000 fishing boat and many thousands of dollars of gear as well. One day, he decided he needed to turn his hobby into a revenue stream, and he hired himself out as a sport fishing guide.

Steven organized a legitimate business, did some marketing, and started to land clients. Eventually, he got to the point where he was pocketing $1,000 or more per trip. Over the course of any given season, he would take home $10,000 profit working weekends for the three months of prime fishing season. Plus, because his boat was now a business asset, he got to write off his boat depreciation and reduce his taxes. Looking at this business like an investor, his $10,000 profit divided by his $50,000 boat investment earned him a healthy 20% annual return on investment. He got to do the hobby he loved and met some amazing people who shared his same passion for fishing. On top of all that, he learned more about fishing as a professional guide in just a few years than he could have learned in a lifetime as a hobbyist. I hope that inspires you to do something similar.

SECRET SHOPPING

Did you know there are companies out there that hire people to be secret shoppers at hotels, restaurants, theaters, etc.? If you like traveling and eating out, you could sign up to be a secret shopper where you are hired to stay at a hotel or eat a meal and then make a thorough professional review of your experience. Most of the time, these companies do not pay you a salary, but they do cover all your expenses in exchange for your thoughtful review.

I have a friend who is a preferred reviewer for one of these secret shopper companies. She regularly lands gigs to stay in hotels out of town. Not only is her hotel stay free, but her flights and meals are reimbursed as well. It has taken her a few years to prove her skills as a reviewer to get to this level of opportunity, but she enjoys a spontaneous and exciting travel lifestyle almost for free.

The possibilities of generating extra income with your spare time are limited only by your creativity and determination to reach your wealth-building goals.

CHAPTER 7

HOUSE HACK

IF ONLY THE FITTEST SURVIVE, ONLY THE CRAFTIEST THRIVE!

WHAT IS A HOUSE HACK AND WHY DO IT?

I understand that you and your family may be emotionally attached to your current house. You may even live in your "dream house." Perhaps you have called it your "Forever Home." Maybe you're hesitant to uproot the kids and move. I acknowledge that the House Hack step may be really hard on an emotional level for you and your family. Or maybe it will actually be easy for you, but not for someone else in your family. However, the house hack step, above all the other steps in Hacking Your Lifestyle, is the most critical to building serious wealth over the long term. If you're like most people, your home is by far the biggest expense in your personal financial life. Once again, there is no way to hack your way into the wealthy class on an average income if you have an average house with an average mortgage payment. Therefore, you need a house that is better suited to your new investing focus. The easiest and cheapest way to accomplish that is through a house hack.

In case you're not familiar with what a house hack is, it's a creative strategy to make your primary residence generate income. Buying a duplex to live in one unit and rent out the other is one of the most common and simple ways to understand house hacks. I bought my first piece of real estate in 1996 as a freshman in college. It was a plain-Jane duplex with each apartment having two bedrooms, two bathrooms, and a one-car garage. In hindsight, the location wasn't the best, literally on the wrong side of the tracks of town. Nonetheless, it got me started.

I lived on one side and rented out the other. I then charged a roommate rent for the other bedroom in my unit. The rent from my tenant and my roommate almost covered my mortgage payment. I understand you may not be nineteen years old like I was with my first house hack. Maybe you have a spouse and kids, and living in a small duplex or getting a roommate isn't an option. In that case, you'll need to find a property that will better suit your family's needs and still generate good income.

I've done that myself as well. In May of 2020, at the height of the COVID-19 panic, I landed an amazing deal on a house to hack that is in one of the trendiest neighborhoods in town. This time, I was on the right side of the tracks. This house is not only in a great area, but is a suitable place for me, my wife, and our three teenage kids to live. The charming 1938 home has 2,500 square feet with four beds and two baths. The special part about this property is that it has a completely detached 1,150-square-foot, two-bed, two-bath guest cottage on the same lot.

The property is situated on a corner, so the front door of each house faces a different street. Most people don't even know the two homes are on one property, which provided the privacy my wife required and the private yard my kids wanted. With less than $10,000 in remodel costs, I converted the guest house into two short-term rental units, an upstairs one-bed apartment and a separate basement studio. The rent from those two units more than covers the mortgage and utilities on the whole property!

If you rent instead of own, my advice is still to purchase a property that you can house hack. The good news for you is getting out of a rental lease is usually cheaper, and possibly easier, than going through the process of selling a house. The worst-case scenario is you pay the break-lease fee or wait for the lease to expire. Another option might be to ask your landlord to let you sublet your apartment until the end of your lease. In most cases, I discourage people from renting apartments for the simple principle that your rent is paying off your landlord's mortgage. Owning real estate is the number-one wealth-building tool on earth for most people in most situations. Since you have to pay to live somewhere, you might as well be paying off your own mortgage to do so.

POP-UP DEFINITION

Sublet (or sublease) - Letting is another term for renting or leasing. Therefore, a sublet is renting a property that you are leasing from someone else. Some lease agreements prohibit subletting, so subletting may require special written approval from the property owner.

If you've always thought you could not qualify to buy a house, or even if you have tried in the past and were denied credit, I want to encourage you to make a mental adjustment now. To become an effective investor, you are going to have to acquire a skill of overcoming obstacles to getting what you want. There are two kinds of obstacles. There are obstacles that the institutions in our culture put up to protect themselves from losses, and there are obstacles we fabricate in our own heads. Both need to be studied so we can find a way around them. **If you only take one thing from this whole section on hacking your lifestyle, I want you to take this: Serious investors become professionals at getting around obstacles, especially the ones in our own heads.**

If your mindset is such that you are convinced you're too poor to buy a house, you will never buy a house. Decide today you are going to do whatever it takes to get a house, and you will get a house. Your first step is to set up appointments with at least five local credit unions or banks. Dress nicely and go into those meetings with the mindset that you are going to figure out what it takes to get a mortgage. Talk to each banker and tell them what you want to get, and ask them to tell you what you need to qualify. They will give you minimum income requirements, down payment options, closing costs, loan terms, credit score, etc. Then, getting a loan is as simple as checking off all the boxes on the forms they give you to complete. You may need to pay down debt, increase your income through the strategies in the Hack Your Lifestyle chapters, adjust your purchase price expectation, improve your credit score, or take other actions as well. Once you know what they are looking for, you know the obstacles you have to overcome.

POP-UP DEFINITION

Closing Cost - This refers to the expenses associated with buying or selling an asset such as real estate. Closing costs can range from less than 1% to over 10% of the sale price.

HOW TO BUY A HOUSE HACK

Once you are ready to make your house hack purchase, there are lots of good books on real estate investment strategies that you should consider reading as you are becoming an investor. I constantly have a fresh list of recommended books at www.TheUnexpectedInvestor.com. You should also seek out local real estate agents who have experience buying investment properties. That said, there are a lot of ways you can find a place to live that will generate income.

Aside from the classic duplex option, you can also purchase a triplex (or three-plex). It's the same as a duplex, just with three units. These are less common, but could work really well. You might be surprised that even four-plexes or quadplexes are usually considered residential property (just like single-family homes, duplexes, and triplexes). Therefore, even four-plexes can be purchased with conventional residential home financing just like a single-family home. Typically, the higher the unit count in a property, the lower the per unit cost is, and potentially the higher the cash flow could be.

Prepare yourself that as you start shopping for these multi-unit homes, the price is likely going to be higher than the house you are currently in. Don't let that sticker shock stop you. Mortgage lenders will give you credit for at least a portion of the rent you will make in the additional unit or units when qualifying you for the loan from an income perspective. In other words, the income from your job is not the only factor when determining how much you can afford when buying a multi-unit property as it would be for a single-family home.

While a duplex, triplex, or quadplex will probably be the easiest properties to find, you could also consider getting creative like I did during COVID-19 by hunting for a property that functions as a single-family home with an ADU or that has a space that can split off from the main house to function as a second unit.

POP-UP DEFINITION

ADU - Additional Dwelling Unit. This term is almost universally used by government zoning authorities for secondary living spaces that are typically smaller than the main residence on a given parcel (or home lot).

Most towns have streets lined with older homes that have basements or wings of homes that can be split off with minimal expense and would create a second living unit to rent out. Before you start adding or knocking down walls, get familiar with your local building code to know what work can happen with or without a building permit. Also, talk to licensed contractors to get a feel for what can be done to stay in the good graces of the city officials.

When shopping for your house hack property, you need to analyze the property before making an offer to ensure it will produce what you need. The ultimate goal in the house hack step should be to cover your mortgage and maybe utilities from the income your house hack generates. I strongly encourage you to find a mentor who has purchased investment property to advise you through this analysis process. The best way to find a mentor would be to start a free account at www.TheUnexpectedInvestor.com and find a fellow HACKER who has successfully completed at least one house hack. The skill of buying rental properties that work long-term is not easily learned from watching YouTube videos or reading books. Every real estate market, and indeed, every property, is unique and requires careful analysis.

SHOULD I TRADE MY CURRENT HOME OR KEEP IT?

As you have been reading about house hacking, perhaps you have assumed you would be selling your current home (if you are a homeowner) in order to buy your house hack. There is certainly nothing wrong with this approach, and in normal times under normal circumstances, it would likely be the best course of action. However, we're not in normal times, and chances are you are not in normal circumstances. Specifically, I'm referring to the interest rate environment we find ourselves in in the mid-2020s. As of the date of the publication of this book, 60% of mortgage holders have a home mortgage at or below 4% annual interest rate, and 80% of mortgage holders have a rate below 5%! Since current interest rates are running over 7%, most homeowners are stuck in what's called the rate lock-in effect. In most cases, selling a home with a mortgage under 5% just doesn't make any sense when rates are anywhere near 7%.

To visualize how dramatic a difference a few percentage points makes on a mortgage, take a look at the two scenarios below for the first loan payment on a thirty-year fixed mortgage:

	3.5% Interest Rate Loan	7.0% Interest Rate Loan	Difference
Loan Balance	$300,000.00	$300,000.00	SAME
Monthly Interest Payment	$875.00	$1,750.00	$900 or 103% Higher
Monthly Principal Payment	$472.13	$245.91	$226.22 or 48% Lower
Total Debt Service Payment	$1,347.13	$1,995.91	$648.78 or 48% Higher

Even though the monthly payment is only 48% higher when the interest rate doubles, a significantly higher percentage of the total payment is going to interest and, therefore, not principal. As we'll see in the "Cash Is King Investing" section, principal loan paydown is one of the rocket boosters propelling us into the wealthy class. Higher interest rate mortgages diminish the power of that booster.

If you find yourself in the rate lock-in effect, you should figure out if your current home could generate enough rent to cover your mortgage and the other expenses associated with running a rental property. If it can, maybe it's time to accelerate your real estate investing career by buying a second home as your house hack and keeping your current home as your first rental.

HOUSE HACK STRATEGY

If you do decide to sell your current home and it nets you enough cash, I suggest you put a 20% down payment on your new house hack purchase. At least 20% down enables you to get rid of mortgage insurance, which typically adds 1% to your interest rate. Also, paying 20% down enables you to weather almost any economic storm that might decrease the value of your house. Having a 20% equity cushion means you'll not likely be stuck in a situation where you can't sell and pay off your mortgage. I know the 2008 housing crash cut more than 20% off most homes, but it's vital to understand that the 2008 crash was the most severe housing crash since the Great Depression in the 1930s.

While a crash of that magnitude could happen again, the chances are small. However, even if housing values fall more than 20%, so long as your income is sufficient to pay the bills, you won't need to sell anyway, making the price reduction of minimal importance in the short term. If any of this seems risky or scary to you, remember, as investors, we live with a constant amount of risk and learn how to manage that risk responsibly. "Nothing ventured is nothing gained" is an old proverb that essentially teaches that the only way to get ahead is to take some risk. I would be the first one to warn you against taking blind or speculative risks. I am, however, challenging you to take measured or calculated risks on a regular basis. A house hack is a low-risk way to learn how to take smart, measured risks that could bring massive rewards.

Now comes the best part. Hunting for real estate is one of my favorite things to do. The mix of fear, excitement, wonder, curiosity, and discovery are all swirling around at the same time, which is exhilarating. If you're nervous and uncomfortable as you start hunting, you're normal. Allow yourself to relax and enjoy the process. Once you get past the newbie jitters and get rid of some of your limiting beliefs, buying real estate can be among the biggest adrenaline rushes on earth. The surest path to building wealth is learning how to embrace the discomfort of using your money for something other than spending.

Before we move on to the next hack, let's summarize the power of the House Hack step on your future net worth. Let's assume you are currently paying $2,000 out of pocket for your mortgage, property taxes, homeowner's insurance, and utilities. If you hit a home run on your house hack, you can completely eliminate your housing costs. Just to be conservative, however, let's assume that after your house hack income, you can reduce your out-of-pocket expenses to just $500 per month. If you take that $1,500 per month reduction in living expenses and invest it over the course of twenty-five years and are able to generate a 9.7% annual return on your investment, your net worth will grow by $1,692,307 just from your house hack!

CHAPTER 8

THE THREE STEPS TO CREDIT CARD HACKING MASTERY

DO YOU WANT TO SAVE MONEY OR LIVE LARGE? YES, THANK YOU VERY MUCH!

What is the most epic vacation you can imagine? Would it be flying business class to spend a week in Dubai at one of the nicest hotels in the world? How about a three-week trip to Egypt to see the 5,000-year-old pyramids? Or what about a week in Israel taking a private tour of the ancient Jewish, Christian, and Muslim sites? If one of these is your idea of an amazing vacation, you're not thinking big enough! A dear friend of mine, David Morrison, once did all those things and more in a "around-the-world" mega-vacation. Literally, his itinerary circumnavigated the planet, landing in some of the most iconic places on earth.

All told, David's trip was to eight world-class destination cities, flying business class the entire way, always staying in five-star hotels (or in lay-flat business-class airplane beds) for forty-five nights straight. His epic odyssey started in Boise, Idaho. From there he flew to Rio de Janeiro, Brazil; to Cairo, Egypt; to Tel Aviv, Israel; to Amman, Jordan; to Dubai, UAE; to Doha, Qatar; to Nepal; and finally to Hong Kong, China, before jetting back home to Idaho. The best part of this story… the whole trip was 100% free. He cashed in over 1,400,000 credit card incentive points in the form of flights, hotels, and cash for this epic trip. As if the "around-the-world" trip isn't enough, David takes epic trips every year, all for little or no cost.

In this chapter, I will shed some light on how this was possible and get you started on your credit card hacking mastery journey. My goal with this hack is to help you live a rewarding and abundant life, even as you gain control of your spending and kick-start an aggressive investing plan. With a little effort and time spent on tracking and deal hunting, you can generate impressive rewards quickly. However, before we get over our skis, literally, we need to back up a little and lay a healthy, sustainable foundation for credit card usage. We'll get back to the world-class vacations and free cash soon, I promise.

We all know that credit card companies offer loyalty incentives, purchasing convenience, and payment flexibility. But we also know that these come at a significant cost in the form of high interest rates. Typically, credit cards charge anywhere from 15% to 25% interest on unpaid balances. It's easy to shake our fists at the banks charging those rates and claim that they are fleecing its users. However, it's important to realize that the banks are extending their users credit that isn't "secured" by anything other than the users' word that they will repay. The credit card company knows that a certain percentage of less responsible users will never pay their balance. The high interest rate ensures that the credit card companies can offer their truly amazing service, cover those losses, and still make a profit. The good news is, however, that you can beat the credit card company at their own game.

You can leverage their incentives, convenience, and flexibility and not only pay zero in interest, but actually get paid by the credit card company to use their product. The ONLY way to accomplish this is to never carry a balance owed past the statement due date.

CREDIT CARD HACK STEP ONE: PAY OFF YOUR CREDIT CARD BALANCES

Now that you have adopted a minimalist mindset, hacked your transportation, converted your hobbies into side hustles, and completed your house hack, you should have enough cash stashed and new income coming in to either completely pay off your credit card balances or create a plan to do so in short order. Regardless of where you are in the process, it is imperative that you create a singularly focused plan to completely eliminate all of your credit card balances (and any other consumer debt) that are interest bearing. A word of wise caution: don't advance to the "Cash Is King Investing" step until you've completely eliminated your credit card debt.

To prove to you why it's essential that you eliminate credit card debt, let's compare the cost of credit card debt to a successful investment strategy. Most seasoned investors are content with an average annual return on investment (ROI) of 10%. Of course we all strive to beat that number, but any active investor who consistently gains 10% per year will grow massive wealth over time. You don't need to be a finance wizard to understand that investing money before you pay off those high-interest accounts makes no sense. While there's no guarantee you'll earn a positive return on your investments year after year, there is a 100% certainty that the credit card companies will take their 20% like clockwork. Unfortunately, human nature has a tendency to ignore the obvious perils of carrying credit card balances. I urge you to shift your mentality to that of an investor and pour all of your available cash and free cash flow into paying off your high-interest debt.

At this point in our wealth-hacking journey, I have to tip my hat to Mr. Dave Ramsey. Dave has built a very successful movement around the idea of paying off credit card debt. One of his signature profile pictures is of him holding a credit card and a pair of cartoonishly oversized scissors, milliseconds away from cutting it in half and tossing it in the garbage. Dave's schtick is that credit cards (along with all debt) are bad and must be eliminated completely. I don't agree with Dave's "all debt is bad" in its purest form.

Where Dave and I do agree is that high-interest credit card balances are bad and must be eliminated immediately. You see, I hold the belief that human beings are actually pretty smart and totally capable of learning how to set spending limits once they understand why it's so important.

Unless you don't trust yourself to set limits on spending and stick to them, the last thing we want to do is cut up our credit cards. In fact, we want more (paid-off) credit cards rather than fewer. More on that later. Once you have paid off your credit cards or have a solid plan in place to do so, it's time to advance to step two: keeping your credit cards paid off forever.

CREDIT CARD HACK STEP TWO: AUTOPAY YOUR STATEMENT BALANCE FOREVER

Perhaps you have met someone who goes on a strict diet every January. After a gluttonous November and December, they cold-turkey stop eating fried food and sugar and start eating mountains of salad and drinking gallons of water. Initially, they lose weight really fast. They look and feel great and aren't shy about telling everyone about it. How many of those friends fall off the wagon and gain all the weight back plus some by March? I was a member at Gold's Gym for a couple of years, and I noticed how magically crowded the gym got every year on January 2, only to return back to normal crowds by Valentine's Day.

The same thing can happen to you with your credit cards if you don't enter into this process with a plan and the determination to work the plan. The temptation to spend more than you make is as difficult as it is for a man not to eat a whole cake after starving for a couple of months. Your budget, which we'll discuss in detail in the Allocation Budget step, needs to comfortably cover your living needs so that you aren't so strapped that you fall off the wagon and rack up credit card balances again.

The best way to keep your credit cards paid off is to log into your credit card accounts and set them all to automatically debit your bank account for the full statement balance every month with no end date. All the credit card companies offer this option. Once you've set this up on all of your credit cards, make a commitment to yourself that you will NEVER turn off that service. This will force you to hold your spending back and ensure that your bank balance can cover your looming credit card bill. Your ability to keep your credit card balances at zero will determine your success in hacking into the wealthy class.

Before we progress to the last and most fun step of credit card hacking mastery, I want to introduce you to a philosophical idea that is critical for you to internalize: "Wealthy people buy luxuries last." Most people who overspend on their credit cards tend to be buying unnecessary luxuries. Spending an extra $100 at the grocery store is less likely to push you over budget. But for wealth-building investors, spending $1,000 on a new TV at Best Buy is like a swimmer wearing a weighted vest in the pool. People who have prioritized building wealth have an instinct that resists making purchases that slow down the wealth-building process.

20% credit card interest is a brake pedal to building wealth. **Start acting wealthy now and buy luxuries last. You will know when it's time to allow yourself to buy luxuries when your investing goals and your spending needs are both being met, and you still have cash left over.**

Credit Card Hack Step Three: Print Points

I know the process of putting steps one and two into practice is hard and unpleasant. Assuming you've accomplished those first two steps or have a plan in place to do so, now comes the almost unbelievable reward of printing points. Point printing will enable you to take world-class vacations, fly regularly for free, and even put thousands of dollars in your pocket every year. This is all possible through leveraging the "loyalty" programs offered by most credit card companies. It's totally legal, and the process of grinding out points can even be fun.

Chances are, you are already using credit cards that generate points or cash-back rewards and you get a free flight or two each year or 2% cash back on fuel or something like that. If that's you, great! However, I am going to expose you to an entire rogue (but totally legal) industry of credit card point printers who have figured out how to live large, all paid for by the credit card companies and the merchants they partner with. As a wealth hacker, this hack helps ensure you can maintain a fulfilling lifestyle even as you establish your 50/40/10 "investment-focused" budgets that we'll talk about in the next HACKER method step.

My globe-trotting friend David Morrison spends an average of $85,000 annually on his credit cards, and from that generates the equivalent of between $20,000 and $40,000 every year in cash, flights, hotel stays, and other freebies. Even living by your 50/40/10 budget, you can "print" a five-figure credit card hack as well! To understand how this is even possible, you must understand why the banks that issue credit cards and the merchants they partner with would be willing to give us thousands of dollars every year.

First of all, your credit card issuer is hoping you will eventually carry a balance and pay them gobs of interest. They assume that almost everyone will find themselves in a pinch at some point and will fall back on credit cards to help them weather the storm. So, credit card companies are patient enough to allow you to accumulate and use rewards because odds are you will eventually start accumulating an interest-bearing balance. The Consumer Financial Protection Bureau claims that Americans pay credit card companies an eye-popping $120 billion each year in credit card interest and late fees.

However, interest and late fees alone aren't the only motivation for credit card companies to reward you for using their cards. Every time a card is swiped or entered into an online shopping cart, the merchant that runs your card pays the credit card company another 1% to 3% of that sale, and sometimes a small flat fee as well. UpgradePoints.com estimates that the total amount spent on credit cards annually is $4.6 trillion. Assuming the average credit card transaction charge is 2% of that $4.6 trillion, an additional $92 billion goes to the credit card companies just from transaction fees! This is where the loyalty program freebies start to make sense. Even if you are among the minority who never pay interest by paying off your balance every month, you are generating transaction fees for the credit card company every time you shop.

You might be wondering why a merchant would be willing to pay the credit card companies 2% of their sale. Merchants know that consumers spend far more money on credit cards than they do when they use cash. According to the Federal Reserve Bank of Boston, a study from October 2016 found that the average consumer cash purchase was $22 compared to $112 for non-cash (debit or credit card). If you've ever run a retail business, you know that volume is usually the name of the game. So, selling five times more on credit versus cash is well worth the 2% fee. Developed countries are diverging further away from cash transactions every year. Consumers have grown to rely on the convenience of using credit cards for lots of reasons, and businesses want to appeal to consumers' preferences.

There's one additional facet to the loyalty programs. Many banks offer a simple cash-back reward system, but some also have partnered with other brands to make their loyalty program more attractive to users and also generate commissions for the credit card company. The most common partnership is with airlines. The partnership between credit card companies and airlines is so ubiquitous that sometimes we interchange the word points with "miles," even if our card doesn't offer airline "miles" credits. Aside from airlines, there are reward systems for hotels, gasoline, cruise lines, and groceries, among others. These businesses also win from your credit card spending by luring you into doing repeat business with them versus their competitors. For example, I am often willing to pay more for a Delta flight than for another carrier because the incentives to use my Delta American Express card offer me luxury perks that other carriers don't. This translates into higher profit margins for both Delta and American Express.

The credit card companies know about point printers. Some of them have taken steps to curb point printing. However, these companies are often willing to take a loss to the tune of thousands of dollars every year because you and I are a tiny minority of their customers. The loyalty incentives that we exploit are necessary for them to attract the vast majority of their highly profitable customers. The average cardholder pays interest, late fees, cash advance fees, annual fees, and merchant transaction fees, as well as generates branded partnership commissions. We're merely gamifying their own system to our advantage.

Point Printing Ground Rules

Now that we understand why banks are willing to allow us to print points, I want to establish a few ground rules before we get into the details:

- **No New Spending!** First and foremost, you must make a pledge to yourself to never spend money that you wouldn't already spend in order to get points. This would cancel out the entire premise of the HACKER method and set you back from your long-term investing goals. Don't become the statistic every credit card company expects you to become by spending more than you need to just due to the convenience of the plastic!

- **Respect Step Two!** Whenever you set up new credit cards, set them to automatically pay the entire statement balance every month. You cannot win with points and pay the high-interest rates charged by these credit card companies at the same time. The banks know that chances are you'll start off intending to pay the balance off, but eventually start accruing a balance. Don't pay the credit card companies! Make them pay you!

- **Always Read The Offer Details!** I am going to reference specific card offers sparingly because the terms change all the time. So it's important to fully understand the terms of the offers from each credit card at the time you apply. Sometimes the annual fees make it a bad deal. In many cases, credit card companies limit you to only open a specific card once in your lifetime. Just make sure you've carefully considered the cost versus reward for each card before you apply.

- **Be Organized!** In order to print massive amounts of points, you must stay organized. Create a spreadsheet or subscribe to an app that tracks important metrics like annual fee amount and renewal date, credit limit, new account incentive requirements, autopay date, etc. You can make a mess of your credit and bank accounts if you don't keep tight control on your accounts. If you know yourself and cannot stay organized enough to do this, my suggestion is for you to take the credit card hack out of your wealth building strategy. The risk of accumulating interest or fees is just too high.

- **Don't Pay More To Use Your Card (Usually)!** Unless you are working toward a lucrative initial incentive spend requirement, most cards don't offer more than 2% cash back. So if your local auto repair shop charges an extra 2.5% to accept your credit card, either ask them to reduce or waive that fee or pay cash instead.

- **Be Ethical!** Don't lie on your credit card applications or say inaccurate things to their agents on the phone. Not only do you want a clean conscience, but you want to avoid credit card fraud as well.

Point Printing Methods

With all of that out of the way, let's fire up the point-printing machines. There are essentially four primary ways to print credit card points, which I outline below. They are often nuanced and a bit complex, and no two people will attack credit card hacking the same way. So, it might be a good idea to read through each one a few times to get familiar with them as you set up your strategy. I also want to disclose right now that what you will read below is merely scratching the surface of this hack. There are thousands of pages of information out there on this subject.

1. New Credit Card Incentives

The most lucrative and quickest way to print points is to sign up for new credit card offers to get their New Member Sign-up Bonus. Almost all credit card issuers offer some sort of incentive to lure new cardholders into their interest and fees profit machine. Some are more lucrative than others, and some may be more appealing to you than to the next person.

Almost all new card incentives tie your reward to your immediate use of their card. A common requirement is that you spend $3,000 in the first three months of holding the card. Once you meet their spending requirement and do so within their time limit, your points total gets credited to your reward account. Once the points are in your reward account, it is usually up to you to log into your account and redeem those points. Each reward system is different, but usually you can get a check mailed to your house, apply the value to your credit card balance, buy airline tickets or hotel stays (more details below), or even get a gift card from places like amazon.com.

To determine the exact value of a given offer, look at their redemption offerings to see how many points it takes to get a gift card or a domestic flight. The current conventional wisdom is that one credit card point is usually worth about one cent. So, to do a rough and dirty assessment of the value of a sign-up bonus, move the decimal two places to the left and convert it to dollars. For example, if a company is offering a 30,000-point bonus, that's worth roughly $300. An aggressive campaign that offers a 100,000-point bonus could be worth about $1,000.

I just recently opened two Chase Business Unlimited Visa cards for two of my companies. The sign-up bonus offered $900 cash back after spending $9,000 within the first three months. I used the cards to pay for a remodel on one of my new rental properties, immediately paid off the balances, and pocketed $1,800 cash. My total time invested in this point-printing deal was less than a half hour. I understand that if you are just getting started, you won't be able to meet the $18,000 spend requirement of this specific deal. However, if you commit to the HACKER method, you'll get there soon enough!

Some companies have rules on how many of their cards you are able to hold at one time. That said, you can multiply your point printing by opening multiple new cards through multiple issuers each year. I have a friend who is an active point printer and has over 70 open credit cards to his and his wife's names. I don't suggest you go out and open 70 accounts tomorrow. Open one or two to get started, and then as you get comfortable with how to master the process, create a schedule to keep opening more accounts.

- The upside - A two-adult household can print one million points or more every single year if organized and spend the time to do the research. Most of these points come from new card sign-up bonuses.
- The downside - Every time you open a credit card, your credit report shows a new hard inquiry, which has a slightly negative effect on your credit. Hard inquiries remain listed on your credit report for two years, but only affect your credit for one year. The good news is, however, that you can largely offset this negative by keeping your credit card balances low. If you keep your total credit card balances at or below 30% of your combined credit limit, your credit score will actually improve.
- Bottom line annual value - The simple "one cent per reward point" rule means that one million points could be worth

$10,000. Some incentive programs, however, offer better conversion rates if you use your points with their preferred brands. Some airlines, for example, offer a point rate above one cent per dollar spent if you're using your points to book flights on their airline. The cherry on top is that this income is tax free to you.

2. Ongoing Spending Incentives

The only credit cards you should ever have in your wallet are ones that offer some form of loyalty reward system. I would suggest you stick with rewards of at least 1.5% of your spending as a minimum. As you use your cards for normal everyday purchases, you continue to rack up points for future redemption.

To go next level on this hack, spend some time seeking out credit cards that incentivize a higher point haul when you spend money on certain categories. For example, some cards will pay up to five times more points for all purchases at grocery stores. Others will offer three times more points if you use their card to pay your internet bill. Others will offer a higher cash-back reward on all your gasoline purchases.

Of course, all of the travel-themed cards will give you mega bonuses for using their card on their products and services. Your Delta American Express will give you double the points for a Delta flight and a free checked bag, for example. In fact, certain Delta American Express cards help you earn MQM (Medallion Qualifier Miles) points on top of your standard reward points. MQM points help you qualify for Delta's Medallion frequent flier program, which awards first-class upgrades, free drinks, priority check-in, and boarding, among other perks.

I have accumulated enough MQMs from Delta to qualify for their top-tier Diamond Medallion for the next two years without spending another dollar with Delta or flying a single flight. Most of those MQMs have come from my credit card spend incentive boosts. Not only do I almost always fly first class for free, I also get amazing perks every year that are worth approximately four free flights.

Once you've obtained and organized your cards based on the spending category bonuses, label each card with the category it's best for. A label maker or even a small strip of paper with clear tape over it is sufficient. Make sure your label isn't opposite the mag strip or security chip so it doesn't get rubbed off with use. Then pull out the grocery incentive card at the grocery store, the airline card when buying flights, the fuel card when buying gas, and so on. While I know it gets cumbersome to carry lots of cards, it's worth it to figure out how to maximize your spending based on the incentivized bonuses. Done right, instead of generating one point (or one cent, which equals 1%) for every dollar spent, you can net three, four, or five times that.

- The upside - A two-adult household can cut their operating budgets by three percent or better and begin to enjoy some of the luxury perks like first-class airplane tickets.
- The downside - So long as you're not spending more than your budget and not paying credit card interest, the only downside to this hack is having to carry around multiple cards and spend the time it takes to be organized enough to always use the best card for each expense type.

3. Airlines, Hotels & Cruises

The fiercest competition for credit card loyalty seems to be in the travel industry. Perhaps that is because the very idea of free travel is very alluring to their customers. Cardholders may be more likely to spend money to obtain free vacations than they would be for cash-back rewards, even if the real value of getting cash back was worth more than the travel. It's also possible that people who are drawn to travel have a higher spend profile or perhaps come back to those brands more frequently. There's also the cross-marketing value of two brands marketing to each other's customer base, which brings value to both companies involved.

For all those reasons, the travel industry often throws out some of the most enticing sign-up bonuses out there. My suggestion is to only jump on airline incentives that offer 70,000 or more points, or hotel cards that offer the equivalent of at least three free nights in a premium hotel for their sign-up bonus. With just a little bit of patience, you'll see these offers all the time.

Another way to cash in on travel is to sign up for new cards when you are planning your normal annual vacation. Let's say you've decided to go on a cruise. Before you start shopping destinations, cruise lines, or even dates, start searching for cruise-branded credit cards that can offer you a really attractive sign-up bonus. With a little luck, you might get a free or deeply discounted vacation on the high seas. Last year, I had a Carnival-branded Mastercard that had generated enough points from the sign-up bonus and a couple months of normal spend to pay for half the cost of a six-night Alaskan cruise for my family of five.

- The upside - Wealth hacking demands strict adherence to tight budgets, but credit card incentives enable us to travel better than most.
- The downside - To maximize your travel bonuses, you must be highly organized and constantly watching out for offers that make epic travel either free or steeply discounted. Also, beware of unexpected fees at premium hotels. Your free stay at five-star hotels may not be truly free if you get stuck with

expensive parking fees, ridiculous breakfast buffet charges, or other such hidden costs.

· Bottom line annual value - The most organized and creative credit card hackers will never pay for another flight, hotel, or major travel expense again. While you do have to pay the applicable travel taxes for these services, you don't have to pay income taxes on the value of the rewards.

4. New Bank Account Incentives

The fourth and final credit card point-printing hack is admittedly not related to credit cards at all. However, it functions essentially the same way and requires the same organization and hunting skill as credit card point printing, so we'll allow it to tag along in this chapter. Just like credit card companies make money from people using their credit cards, banks make money when you deposit your money with their institution. Similar to credit card companies, banks make their money on interest and fees. When a bank account holder deposits money in a bank account, the bank then loans a portion of that money out to someone else, which generates interest for the bank. Overdraft fees, ATM fees, bounced check fees, monthly statement fees, and so on are other ways banks make money off each account. Therefore, banks have a very similar desire to entice people to open bank accounts and do so with lucrative sign-up bonuses.

Where credit card companies require you to spend a certain amount of money to redeem a sign-up bonus, banks usually require you to either maintain a minimum balance and/or set up an automatic monthly deposit into the new account. Their hope is that you have your employer set up your paycheck to automatically deposit and become a permanent account holder. The truth is, however, that any kind of automatic transfer will work most of the time.

The typical bank account offering will give you a cash bonus of anywhere from $100 to even as much as $600 just for opening an account and jumping through their hoops. As I am writing this, U.S. Bank is offering a $600 sign-up bonus if you deposit $25 into a Bank Smartly Online Checking account and complete two direct deposits of $5,000 each over the course of the first three months of owning the account. There is no rule that says you have to keep your money in the account for a certain time, and as soon as you receive the reward, you are free to close the account if you want.

Let's walk through a return on investment formula to show how lucrative this hack can be. If you time everything optimally, you are going to need $5,000 to be tied up for a while to make this one work. Transfer $5,000 into this new account on the 15th of the month, then on the 1st of the following month, pull it back out, then re-transfer it again the following 15th. Then you have met the bank's requirement and get $600 automatically deposited into that account. To keep the math simple, let's say you had your $5,000 "invested" in this incentive for a full thirty days. Your total ROI on the project was $600 / $5,000 = 12%, and it only took a month.

Think this through to the next level, and imagine transferring the same $5,000 from bank to bank, constantly generating new account incentives. With enough organization and time hunting for the best offers, your $5,000 "investment" could conceivably multiply several times over year after year

- The upside - Bank account incentives generate real money with minimal complication.
- The downside - Again, this hack requires a high level of organization and patience. It also takes a sizable chunk of money out of your daily use. Additionally, some smaller banks are a bit of a hassle to deal with, so some offers

may not be worth the effort. Also note that most banks will treat this bonus as interest and, therefore, it will be taxable income.

- Bottom line annual value - A well-organized bank account hacking operation can yield as much as 100% returns year after year. While each person's strategy will vary, it's reasonable to generate $5,000 or more every year by opening accounts that offer strong sign-up bonuses.

Smart Ways To Meet Spend Requirements

As we wrap up this chapter, I want to reinforce the idea that it's vital for the wealth hacker to be the smartest "consumer" out there. Undisciplined consumers spend more than they make on stuff they don't need. Smart consumers take advantage of the interest-bearing and fee-generating land mines the big credit card companies and banks set for the typical consumers.

Smart consumers sign up for and land lucrative bonuses by spending only what they would have spent anyway. They never let credit card balances accumulate, never pay interest, and never pay a premium to a vendor just to use their credit card. That said, you might be wondering how you can possibly get your credit card spending high enough to meet these spending requirements. Here are a few suggestions:

- **Restaurants** - When you are out to eat with friends, you always pay on your card and they give you cash. Just make sure the cash is in your hand or Venmo account before you swipe.
- **From Debit to Credit** - Look at your checking account statement and find recurring transactions that might accept a credit card without charging you more and switch those charges to your credit cards. Oftentimes the HOA, local gym,

water, power and gas companies, among others will gladly automatically charge your credit card without charging more than if you pay cash.

· **Homeowner's Insurance** - Ask your mortgage company if they will let you pay your homeowner's insurance on your credit card instead of through your mortgage.

· **Family Trips/Reunions** - If your entire family vacations together, offer to be the flight and lodging coordinator and put the whole thing on your card. Be sure to secure payment in cash from your family members before you lock in their ticket.

· **Corporate Reimbursement** - If you work for a company that gives you authority to spend on its behalf, use your own credit card and request reimbursement rather than using the corporate card.

· **Real Estate Investing** - As discussed in the HACKER Method step: Cash is King, one of the best ways to build wealth is by investing in real estate. Almost all real estate requires some remodel and has recurring expenses that can be paid for on credit cards. This above all other categories is how I amass ridiculous amounts of credit card points.

· **Business Spending** - If you convert your hobbies into side hustles or if you decide to launch any other kind of business, put as much of your corporate spending on cards as possible and see your points balance skyrocket. Another good thing about most credit cards opened in the name of your business is that they don't report your card usage to your personal credit report.

· **Become a Travel Concierge** - This may seem like a stretch and even a bit random, but I know a guy who makes over $300,000 every year working about twenty hours per week serving as a personal travel concierge for a billionaire family. As a travel agent, hotels kick back a percentage of the stay to him and every flight, hotel, meal and souvenir is purchased on one of his cards and he prints points by the millions. I know coming across billionaire families isn't something we can plan our future around, but perhaps something like this on a smaller scale could be a way for someone just getting started could print some serious points. One realistic example of this would be to volunteer to be the travel planner for your local church or community group. Many churches plan out of town trips every year. Mission trips to Africa, high school camp at the lake, hurricane relief in Florida are just some of the things that you could volunteer to manage. The travelers give you the money for their travel, then you pay for everything on your cards. This will enable you to rack up massive points while providing an appreciated service for a good cause. Just make sure you are paid by the traveler before you use your card!

If you are serious about firing up your point-printing enterprise, I strongly suggest you find your go-to source for ongoing point-printing research. The two sources I have come to trust are The Doctor of Credit and The Points Guy, but there are others out there to be found with a Google search. Aside from Google Sheets, I also like to use the Mint app and AwardWallet to keep my accounts and points balances organized. Wallethub.com estimates there are 1.25 billion active credit card accounts in the world today. The cool thing is, you only need about fifty and a couple spare hours each week to generate a five-figure salary for yourself and your family.

If you are still reading this, you've made it past the most radical part of the HACKER Method's concepts. The next steps will still challenge your instincts. However, if you've allowed yourself to accept the challenge to hack your lifestyle, the rest of the steps will get incrementally easier to implement.

HACKER SECTION 2

ALLOCATION BUDGETING

CHAPTER 9

LAVISHLY LIVING ON LESS

IN FLEETING PASSION'S WAY, MINDFUL HEARTS FIND TREASURES MEANT TO STAY.

A WORLD CLASS HONEYMOON

I woke up on Valentine's Day 2004 as a single man for the last time. By 3 p.m. that day, I was married to my dream girl, Jill Bramhall. I knew early on that she was the one. I played it cool for as long as I could, but finally popped the question just four months after we started dating. Those first four months FLEW by, and almost everything about it was magical. After flying high for four months, I expected the euphoric feelings to continue. But they didn't. The following seven months of engagement felt like they stretched on for an eternity.

Don't get me wrong, things with Jill and I were good and getting better. The problem was me. Once I make a decision, I am driven to action. So, it drove me crazy to "decide" to get married and then just wait.

About three months into being engaged, I had to do something to keep my mind occupied. While Jill was planning the wedding, I decided to start planning our honeymoon. Since we had four whole months to go, I went a little overboard on the details. I had pages and pages of notes, calendars, local tips, flight times, and maps of the attractions and restaurants we were going to visit. I even created a countdown spreadsheet that automatically counted the weeks, days, hours, and minutes remaining to the moment we were going to leave the church as husband and wife. It was going to be a honeymoon for the ages!

My wife worked very hard organizing our wedding, and it showed. It was truly epic. We had two ministers, a sixteen-person wedding party, singers, a pianist, a harp player, several volunteers, and about 300 guests. Every detail was purposefully thought through, and the ceremony went off without a hitch. As we were leaving the church, I was not only ecstatic to start my life married to Jill, but I was also excited to serve Jill as she had served us both through the wedding ceremony. My carefully crafted, world-class, two-week honeymoon in Orlando, Florida, had begun!

I planned that honeymoon with the goal of creating powerful memories for both of us. I remember taking one last look over my plans the day before the wedding and wondering which aspect of our trip would be the most memorable for Jill. Would it be the surprise love notes, flowers, and gifts? Would it be our luxury resort and its amenities? Would it be the theme parks or tourist attractions? Would it be the dinners with alligator meat and other exotic food? It turns out that none of those things was her most powerful memory. I later learned she was most struck by how carefully we followed a budget. A budget!? It would be a lie to say I wasn't just a little bit crushed and embarrassed at the same time. Did I go overboard and create a bad memory that took away from the whole point of our first trip together? Was I too stingy? Did we miss out on something important because of my incessant cost controls?

A few years later, we were talking about the honeymoon budget, and I asked her to clarify. I knew the budget thing was a shock to her, but did it ruin the honeymoon for her? When she realized that I had taken her budget comments as a negative critique, she set the record straight. I was relieved when she affirmed that the honeymoon was in fact world-class, and she loved it! To this day, she still regularly reminds me that she's thankful we have established a smart budgeting lifestyle that has enabled us to accomplish the things we have. She appreciates the fact that we have never violated our budgeting principles, which has directly led to our ability to achieve financial success in spite of living on a low income for much of our married life.

We approached the honeymoon the way we approached everything when we were getting started. First, one of our wedding gifts was two weeks in a timeshare at the Marriott Resort in Orlando, so our destination was picked for us, and our lodging cost us nothing. Second, I cashed in air miles, so our flights cost us a few dollars in taxes. Then, we bought inexpensive breakfast food and brown bag lunch supplies at the grocery store, so we only ate out for dinners. We totally milked the honeymoon thing and regularly got free stuff like desserts wherever we went. We used discount coupons, and even went to a timeshare sales presentation to get free and discounted tickets to several theme parks.

We were young, had no children, and both had jobs. There was no reason why we couldn't have spent lavishly on this trip, and our culture would have told us to do so. You only have one honeymoon, so it's okay to let loose, right? Not if you want to hack into the wealthy class it's not! However, I hope you can see that while we followed a very strict budget and spent a fraction of what most people would spend on a two-week trip to Orlando, we still had an unforgettable, WORLD-CLASS vacation.

I am sharing all of this with you so you realize that living within a budget doesn't mean you have to live a miserable, no-frills life. A little discipline mixed with creativity can make the most budget-conscious events very fulfilling. And of course, the prize at the end of the road will be more than enough reward for the discipline early in your journey. Later in this book, we are going to learn how to create and follow a budget that will ensure you are able to kick-start and sustain a meteoric rise into the wealthy class. But before I get into the nitty-gritty budgeting details, it's important to understand both how and why we spend money, and to see the vision of the effects of long-term budgeting.

TAKE CHARGE OF YOUR HUNTER-GATHERER INSTINCTS

I know that many people recoil at the thought of making and following a budget. For some of you, it's because working with numbers is either confusing or just not fun. For others, maybe you have tried to follow budgets and have given up after time. I understand that creating a budget and sticking to it takes focus, energy, and, above all, discipline. But creating a lifestyle around a very purposeful and carefully planned budget is non-negotiable if you want to hack your way into the wealthy class. It doesn't matter if you earn minimum wage like I did for many years or if you make six figures as a professional. Wealth building requires budgeting.

Budgeting is a necessity for building wealth because we humans have a condition in our brain that fools us into buying things we don't need and can't afford. It's not like we are stupid and just being duped by slick marketers. We know the new iPhone with three rear cameras is not significantly better than the iPhone in our pocket that has only two rear cameras. But we click the "Buy" button or swipe the credit card anyway, knowingly putting ourselves further in debt or using up savings that are intended for something else more important. I've done it too. We all have, and we all know we should get control of these decisions. To overcome our poor spending behaviors, it's important that we first understand why we spend as carelessly as we do.

MIT researcher Vladas Griskevicius reports in Scientific American that our poor spending decisions are a product of biological instincts developed millennia ago when we were hunter-gatherers. Griskevicius explains, "...[there's] a theory from evolutionary biology stating that organisms have to make trade-offs when deciding how to allocate resources (e.g., food, money) in order to maximize reproductive success. Some organisms develop fast strategies characterized by a striving for short-term gains without regard for long-term consequences." In other words, our fast strategies are instinctive, and they push us to use our limited resources to seize upon opportunities as quickly as possible.

Picture a scenario where you are a hunter-gather living 10,000 years ago. You and your clan are starving. It's been three days since any of you have eaten anything more than a few berries. You've been hunting for hours and have used up all but three of your arrows shooting at small prey that have eluded your sharp hunting skills. You finally spot a deer in the forest. You shoot your first arrow but miss. You load the second one, pull back silently, aim, and shoot. You miss again. Thankfully, the deer didn't run off, and you have one last arrow. Do you try a third time even though you will be out of arrows? Of course you do! The survival of your family depends on you making this kill.

Without hesitation, you draw back the last arrow and shoot. You hit him! The deer jolts, walks a few steps, and drops! Your brain is flooded with dopamine and adrenaline because you will bring home enough food to keep your entire clan fed for at least a week. As you bring your kill back to your clan, you victoriously replay the hunt in your mind. Not for one second do you regret using your last arrow. The concept of "shopper's remorse" has never entered your mind. In fact, could you imagine returning to camp with no food and an extra arrow in your quiver? If the chief were to ask you why you returned with an arrow and no food, and you said, "I am saving it for ten years from now so I can retire," you would probably have been kicked out of the tribe.

Our brains today are genetically identical to that of our ancestors from 10,000 years ago. Today, instead of using a quiver of arrows to get what we need, we use money. Unfortunately, we use money today like we used arrows then. We spend our money as soon as we get it (or even sooner), acting as if our survival depends on it. The problem with this kind of behavior lies in the fact that we aren't living in day-to-day survival mode. Most of us are not worried about where our next meal is coming from. Yet, we still spend money as if ten years from now isn't important or will never even come to pass.

As a wealth hacker, you must use your frontal cortex, where logic and long-term planning are created, to overpower your hunter-gatherer fast strategies. You must make every purchase with a clear picture of ten or even twenty years from now in mind. Since I haven't figured out a way to turn off the impulsive desires in my brain, I have determined that the best way to adapt my spending habits is to force my spending to operate within a logical budget. Budgets should be created to intelligently balance your needs and wants as viewed from a long-term wealth-building plan.

Over the last twenty years, I have refined a budget that is uniquely designed to build generational wealth. I call it the 50/40/10 budget. If you fuse the lifestyle hacks in the first HACKER section with a 50/40/10 budget, your wealth will begin to grow almost immediately. If we think of your lifestyle hacks as the foundation of a building, the 50/40/10 budget is the structural frame of the building. If these two concepts are well planned and built, the rest of the HACKER steps can be easily incorporated and set you on your path to significant wealth that will last for generations, regardless of how much your salary is today.

CHAPTER 10

THE 50/40/10 CONCEPT

A PENNY SAVED IS A PENNY LOST TO INFLATION.

It all started with my mom. Mom gave my three siblings and me an allowance for the chores we did around the house. When she paid us, she made us split our individual proceeds up three ways. Half of the money could be used to buy pretty much anything we wanted. But 40% had to go into a savings account, and the last 10% had to be given to the church as a tithe.

This system taught me a valuable skill that I wish everyone had learned. Because I was never able to use all of the money that was technically mine, I got comfortable with capping my spending far below both my income and my bank balance. The practice of immediately splitting the money out trained me to see my money as having multiple purposes and not just as something to spend. Of course, I was tempted to use the money in my savings or giving account to buy toys or candy, but

I learned the discipline to not see those two buckets as a slush fund to satisfy my every whim.

I admit that I abandoned Mom's budget system once I moved out on my own. Like most people, I started earning a paycheck and spent most of what came in. It never occurred to me to keep using Mom's system as an adult. It wasn't until I had kids and set up their chores-for-rewards system that I rediscovered Mom's ingenious method. I remember one time when my wife and I were helping our kids split their money into three ziplock baggies labeled "Spending," "Investing," and "Giving to Change the World." As I stared at the three categories, I had an epiphany. What would happen if we did this in our adult lives with our adult incomes?

My quick math intrigued me enough to open a spreadsheet and chart out a wealth-building plan based on the 50/40/10 budget concept. My eyes first went to the monstrous wealth we could create if we could invest 40% of everything that came into the family accounts. According to my projections, we would be financially independent by the age of fifty-two, when our last kid would turn eighteen.

While the prospect of gaining financial freedom at a relatively young age was very appealing, I admit, however, that the pressure on the spending side was intimidating. At the time, we were earning less than $36,000 per year from our salary and spending every bit of it. Nonetheless, the allure of obtaining financial freedom early in our lives was enough to make the commitment to figure out how to live on 50%. It was here that we perfected many of the lifestyle hacks discussed in the first step, "Hack Your Lifestyle."

My initial projections to be financially free by fifty-two years old were way off, however. We actually quit our salaried jobs six years earlier than planned, and our net worth was more than triple the expected number on the day I quit working for a paycheck.

INVESTING IS LIKE BODYBUILDING

If you were paying attention at the beginning of this chapter, you saw that my mom had me and my siblings put our 40% into a **SAVINGS** account. I'm telling you, however, to put your 40% directly into an **INVESTMENT** account. Saving and investing are similar concepts, but are not synonyms. Let's compare wealth building to bodybuilding. Putting your money in savings would be like taking a twenty-minute stroll through the park every day. Investing your money, on the other hand, would be like an hour of heavy curls, squats, and bench presses every day. Taking a walk isn't bad for you, but it's not going to make you a bodybuilder. Likewise, a savings account is just simply not a wealth builder.

To put it bluntly, putting money in savings is essentially a money-losing waste of time for those of us serious about building wealth and finding financial freedom. You read that right! I just said saving money is a bad idea, and here are the four major reasons why:

1. Saving Money is a Waste of Time...
   No, seriously, it's literally wasting away over time.

No, Seriously, It's literally wasting away over time. Savings accounts almost always offer an interest rate well below the rate of inflation. Therefore, the real value (or purchasing power) of your savings is dropping constantly. Let me explain. If inflation is running at 3.8% and your savings interest rate is 1%, every $100 in your savings account is losing $2.80 of its purchasing power every single year. It's not that the actual balance is decreasing by $2.80, but its buying ability decreases.

Let's use a real-life example: Let's say a nice dinner and a movie cost $100 today. With 3.8% inflation, that same night out should cost $103.80 a year from now if the cost to provide those services increases at the rate of inflation. In that same year's time, $100 in your savings account will have gained only $1 in interest, putting your balance at $101. Even though the bank gave you $1 for "saving" your money with them, you just lost $2.80 in purchasing power.

Losing $2.80 on date night is not the end of the world, but look what happens to your effective inflation-adjusted purchasing power over the course of twenty years:

Assuming inflation is 3.8%
And assuming your savings interest is 1%
And assuming you make $55,000 per year and deposit 40% or
$22,000 every year in savings
And assuming you start out with $25,000 in savings

THEN

You will have deposited a total of $440,000.00
And your savings balance, including compounding interest, will
be $514,923

BUT

The inflation adjusted purchasing power only feels like $365,645 in
today's dollars!
In other words, you LOST $160,278 in purchasing power!

BECAUSE

Dinner and a movie that cost $100 today will cost $203.12
in 20 years!

THEREFORE

Saving money is literally wasting away with time!

1. Savings Accounts Are Too Easy to Rob

Savings accounts are extremely easy to tap into when the temptation or
the need arises. It's extremely difficult to stay disciplined and not spend
money that's sitting there just a few clicks away. Your 40% should go
into an account that is thief-proof. In case you were wondering, the
thief is you! I suggest two practical ways to thief-proof your investment
account. First, put the investment account at a different institution
from where you hold your personal checking and savings accounts. This
usually requires the inconvenience of a few more steps to pull money
out. Second, make your investment account a joint account with your
significant other (or a highly trusted accountability partner) and require
both signatures to draw on it.

2. Savings Accounts Are Really Just Delayed Spending Accounts

As a kid working within my 50/40/10 budget, I never fully understood
the difference between my spending and savings account. In reality, I just
used my savings account to cover the purchases my spending account
couldn't cover. Most of us have at least a vague plan for our savings,
but inevitably dip into it to cover purchases that our checkbook can't
cover. Every time we cheat our long-term plans by making "spending"
purchases with our "savings" account, we are doing serious damage to
our quest to build wealth.

3. A Savings Account Gives A False Sense Of Accomplishment

Cultural pressure to save money makes you think that stashing away money in a savings account is good and gives you a false sense of security. We feel good about ourselves as we slowly and painfully build up a savings balance. The problem with this practice is that we are losing valuable time when our "saved" money could be generating a return well above the rate of inflation, thus building our wealth. Just like people with a poverty mindset see money as something to spend, the middle class sees money as something to save. You're a wealth builder now, and wealth builders see money as something to invest!

LIVING ON AND GROWING YOUR 50%

We'll get into specifics in the next chapter, but for now, we are just talking about the theory of living on 50% of your income. Living on a tight budget, especially for people new to budgeting, is a challenge. Austere financial constraints have the tendency to grind on anyone over time. That is why it is essential that you begin to think about how to increase your 50% spending budget. I am not suggesting you increase the 50% to say, 55%. I am suggesting that you attack the income side of the issue so that 50% is an ever-growing number with growing purchasing power.

The quickest way to increase your spending budget was already detailed in the first HACKER method, "Hack Your Lifestyle." The combination of your house hack, side hustles, transportation hack, and credit card hack should enable you to live well on less. If you really crush the lifestyle hacks, you might be living better on the 50/40/10 budget than you were before starting the lifestyle hacks. It will take a lot of focus and hard work, but it is possible if you'll commit 100%.

In order for your 50% spending bucket to grow steadily and kick off more and more free cash flow, you need to invest your 40% bucket in assets that will both increase in value and produce cash flow over time. I hesitate investing in things like precious metals or cryptocurrency simply for the reason they don't produce cash flow. I also don't loan money out to other people's projects because, while a loan produces interest income (cash flow), the invested money doesn't appreciate.

Let me give you one simple example of how I boosted my 50% spending category by investing my 40% in real estate. In 2015, I had stockpiled $37,000 in my investment account. I decided to buy a rental house from a builder offering a great price to purchase the house before the construction was completed. The house was 1,700 square feet and had three bedrooms and two bathrooms. The house was in a decent (but not stellar) location in Boise, Idaho. I bought it for $185,000.

Seven years later, that house was worth over $430,000! Not only did the house more than double in value, in those same seven years I pocketed over $58,000 profit from rent. Splitting that profit out using the 50/40/10 budget comes out to an average of $345 in my pocket every month, forever. It's also pushing $276 every month back into my investing category, so I can accelerate the wealth-building process.

Once you see this happen one time, you'll be addicted to doing it over and over. The reason I highlight this property specifically is that it is one of my poorest-performing assets. The rest of my assets are usually dumping far more into my spending budget every month. I would not have been able to purchase this house, nor the rest of my cash-producing assets, had I not had the discipline to control my spending up front and prioritize investing long term.

Not only do my cash-producing assets add to my spending category every month, but when I sell an asset, I also get to capture 50% of the profit on the sale and dump it into my spending account. The 40% of the sale profits also recycle into the investment fund, and I make the world a better place by giving away the rest.

THE POWER OF INVESTING 40% OF YOUR INCOME

Making significant contributions to an effective investing strategy over long periods of time has an almost unbelievable result. Below are three realistic scenarios with graphs so you can have a visual understanding of what I am talking about. Each scenario assumes you are following the 50/40/10 strategy and that your starting income increases by 5% each year.

Scenario 1: $14,400 first year investing contribution (40% of $36,000) for 20 years at 10% ROI:

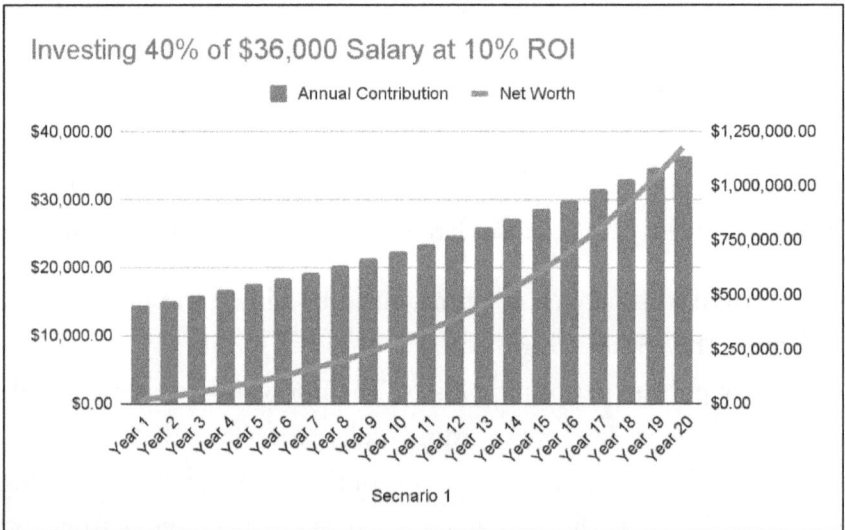

Scenario 2: $20,000 (40% of $50,000) first year Investing annual for 20 years at 15% ROI:

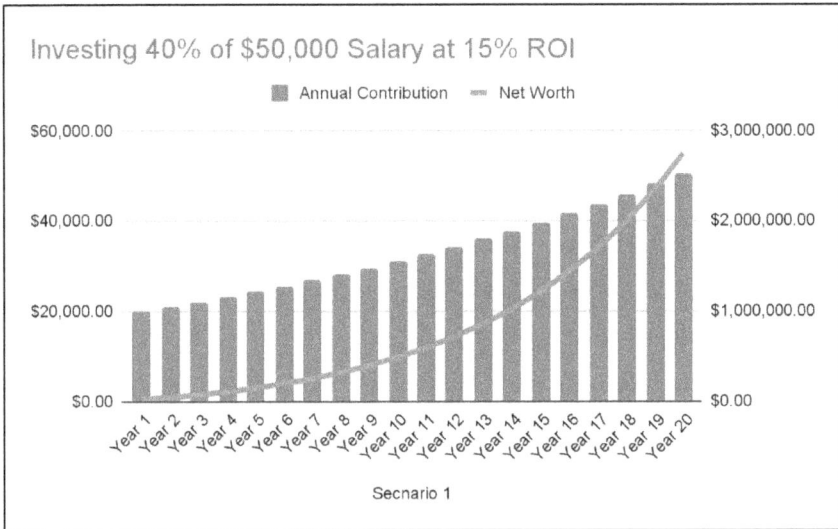

Investing 40% of $50,000 Salary at 15% ROI

Annual Contribution — Net Worth

Secnario 1

Scenario 3: $30,000 (40% of $75,000) first year investing annual for 20 years at 20% ROI:

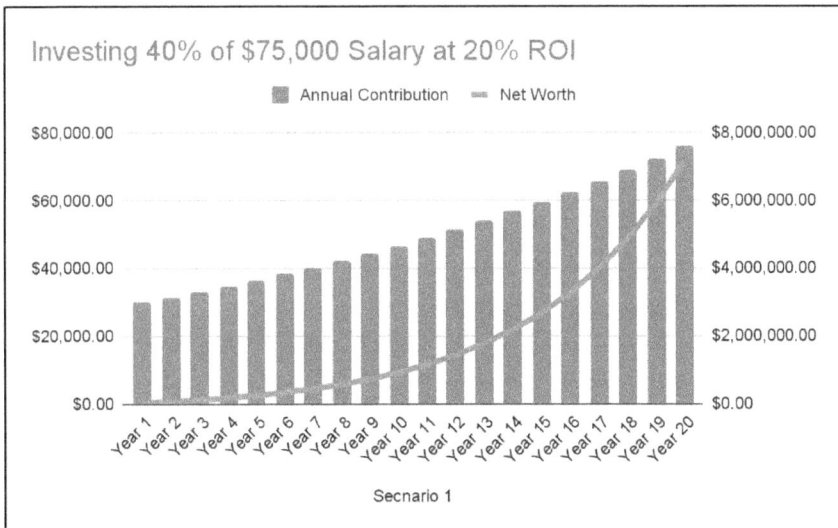

Investing 40% of $75,000 Salary at 20% ROI

Annual Contribution — Net Worth

Secnario 1

My hope is that visualizing a net worth of almost $1,200,000 on the lower end and over $7,000,000 on the higher end is enough to motivate you to engage in this concept. This is not just wishful thinking. As you adopt the HACKER method into your daily life, you too can learn to build significant wealth.

THE SPIN THEOREM

As you process the radical idea of capping your spending at 50% of your income so that you can invest 40% and obtain the net worth illustrated above, I think it's time to introduce you to the SPIN Quotient. The SPIN Quotient is a term I created to help new investors quickly calculate the future value of money when launching 50/40/10 budgets. In other words, the SPIN quotient is a quick way to measure how much it will cost you in long-term investment returns if you spend money out of your investment account instead of investing it.

SPIN simply comes from mashing the first two letters of the words "SPending" and "INvesting" to form SPIN. I want your head to spin every time you face a decision to spend beyond 50% of your income. Another analogy would be that I want you to spin away from spending and toward investing every time you're tempted to cheat the 50% spending limit. That said, you should set yourself up to spend within 50% of your income guilt-free. You have to spend some money to live a dignified life. Only apply the SPIN quotient to keep yourself committed to investing the full 40%.

The SPIN Theorem is:

$$C(1+ROI)^y$$

C = The cost of the item

ROI = your expected average annual return on your investments as a decimal

Y = The number of years in your investing plan

In case high school algebra was a few years ago for you, let me give you an example for how to calculate the SPIN Theorem. I have a weakness for taking my wife out to eat. When my wife cooks at home, she's busy and distracted. But when we're at a restaurant, we're alone, we each get to pick our preferred yummy meal and let the cooks, waitstaff and bussers do the hard work. So if there's an area where I have been tempted to break the 50% spending budget, it's in my dining out budget. So let's run the SPIN Theorem on a nice $100 dinner out.

While I encourage you to plug your own numbers into this formula (or use the free SPIN Theorem calculator at www.TheUnexpectedInvestor. com/calculators), I always use 20% as my expected annual return (ROI). When I first started investing, I had a 20 year investing horizon (y). So my original SPIN Theorem formula for this dinner would have been:

$$\$100 \text{ dinner} \times (1+0.20 \text{ annual return})^{20 \text{ years}} = \$3,833$$

In other words, if we pay for one nice $100 dinner out today from our investing bucket, we will rob ourselves of $3,833 from our long term wealth! I've had some really delicious steak dinners in my life, but I can't think of a single one that would have been worth $3,833!

What if your weakness isn't a $100 dinner out but instead something much cheaper like a candy bar. Maybe you grab a Snickers every week at the checkstand as you are loading your groceries on the belt. If that $1 candy bar is beyond your 50% budget for spending, it's costing you $38.33 off your long term investing goal and it happens every week. Is that candy bar worth $153.32 every month to your future self? What about a more expensive cheat like a $1,000 OLED TV? That would be $38,330 off your goals! Paying $20,000 more for a new car versus a used one costs your future self $766,600!

My best advice for beginning a life within the 50/40/10 budget is to commit to learning the skill I learned as a kid to look at my money as having three distinct uses. Just like bench pressing over and over again will develop your pectoral and tricep muscles, going through the intentional exercise of splitting your income out 50/40/10 and respecting those percentages will develop your investing and charitable donation muscles. If you stick with it over the long term, your brain will become comfortable capping spending at 50% and get a dopamine rush every time you invest your 40%. Not only that, you'll likely find extreme satisfaction in giving money away to make the world a better place too. With that, let's finish this chapter discussing the 10% part of 50/40/10 budgeting.

GIVING AWAY 10% TO MAKE THE WORLD A BETTER PLACE

One of the most important concepts of building wealth is the idea of blessing others with the abundance you have received. Rather than tell you how to do this, I want every person using the 50/40/10 system to come up with their own 10% giving philosophy. I am going to say, however, that it is vital to begin giving away 10% of everything you earn right away. If you are not faithful with a small fortune, you will not "earn" a large one. If you are not able to give away $100 out of every $1000, you will be less able to give away $100,000 out of every million. Just as restricting yourself to spending just 50% of your income takes self-control and intentionality, giving away your hard-earned money also takes an incredible amount of devotion and humility.

Perhaps you already have a passion project that you could continue or start giving to. If not, I suggest you spend some time thinking about an aspect of our world that is underfunded, where your giving could make a huge impact on as many lives as possible. If you can find an organization that is doing truly impactful work, you will have a total flip on your view of giving. You will go from struggling to give the full

10% to holding yourself back from exceeding the 10%. I know a lot of wealthy people who care more about the causes they fund than some of the silly stuff they spend their fortunes on. I don't have any science to back this up, but I think people who are generous with their wealth are far happier than those who are not.

I spent sixteen years as CEO of a non-profit organization. One of my key roles as CEO was fundraising. I've met with people from every economic background in my fundraising efforts. I've talked with the little old widow living on social security, the family with a $100,000,000 charitable trust, and everyone in between. The thing that always surprised me most about asking people to donate their money was how most people were not only willing to give, but usually eager to give. The people I had the privilege to talk to about making the world a better place had found their cause. They knew how they were supposed to give back because they identified the injustice in the world that could be corrected through their generosity.

If you don't yet know what your noble cause is, spend some time meditating about it. Make a list of things in this world that aren't the way they should be. Then research organizations that are attempting to tackle those problems. Go to fundraiser events for those organizations, and let your heart be touched and your mind stimulated by how your money can be used to make the world a better place. You just watch! If you dive in head first, your favorite money category will very likely be the 10% giving category and not the 40%, or even the 50%.

Now that we've established the idea of the 50/40/10 budget, next we'll dig into the structure and application in real life.

CHAPTER 11

THE 50/40/10 STRUCTURE

TEN YEARS AGO WAS THE BEST TIME TO PLANT A TREE. TODAY IS THE SECOND BEST TIME.

HOW INVESTING 40% TRANSLATES INTO BUILDING WEALTH

Purchases with the potential to increase in value or those used in the creation of other items of value are called "Assets" in the finance world. For example, rental real estate, stocks, and bonds are considered assets because they have a strong track record of going up in value and/or generating income over the long term. Other items for personal use like cars, furniture, appliances, and swimming pools generally do not go up in value and usually aren't used to generate income. Therefore, for our purposes, they should be considered expenses or liabilities. Your 40% investment account should never be used to purchase expenses or liabilities. That's what your spending account is for. Remember, as your investments start to grow and generate more and more income, your spending account will grow with it, affording you the ability to buy nicer cars, furniture, etc. within the 50/40/10 system. See the simplified chart below to see which account covers what spending type:

50% Spending Bucket		40% Investing Bucket
Expense	Liabilities or Obligations	Income Producing or Appreciating Assets
Living Expenses	Home Mortgage	Rental Real Estate
Furnishings	Credit Card Balances	Stocks
Vehicles	Auto Loans	Bonds
Subscriptions	Payday Loans	Businesses/Side Hustles
Vacations	Leases	Intellectual Property

OPEN YOUR STOCK BROKERAGE ACCOUNT

A few disclaimers before we go any further. I am not a stockbroker, nor am I a licensed financial advisor. I am not making investing suggestions or giving specific advice on what, when, and where to invest. I'm merely pointing out a generalized strategy on how to grow wealth over the long term. I am also not going to go into depth on the terminology or "how-to" on investing in stocks, real estate, or other asset classes. There are volumes of great material out there that would do a far better job than I. So if you find yourself not understanding terms or not knowing how to proceed, I suggest you seek out other materials to achieve a better overview of those items. Most brokerage firms also have licensed brokers who can help you learn the ropes.

It has become conventional wisdom in the investing world that wealth building through investing exclusively in stocks does not perform as well as other asset classes like real estate or building your own business. However, I feel like the best way to start to think like an investor, especially for someone new to the whole concept of buying assets that increase in value and generate income, is through the purest free market structure on earth: the stock market.

The skills you learn investing in stocks will serve you very well in any other asset class. So, I encourage you to start investing in stocks while your investing balance is small. Once your investing account is large enough and you have some experience investing, I like to see people investing in larger assets such as real estate or small businesses.

To kick off your investing career, my suggestion is to open an account with an established stock brokerage. There are many brokerage funds happy to receive your investment funds, even if you are starting off with a relatively small initial deposit. Do your research and select a firm that offers free or very low-cost trades and has no maintenance fees. Harking back to the chapter on credit card hacking mastery, search for a brokerage account that offers incentives for new accounts so you can print some more benefits in the process.

Once your brokerage account is open, set it up to automatically transfer your 40% investing amount into it every month. You are far more likely to maintain your investing commitment if the transfer is automatic. If you decide to just do it manually every month, you're likely to skip one or two, then just stop doing it all together. If your income varies from month to month, still set up an automatic transfer that is an average of what you expect to make, and adjust the transfer once or twice a year.

I encourage everyone to start buying and selling stocks for four key reasons. First, it's important to see how assets react to the news of the day. Investors need to learn how and why certain stocks will go up or down in value as the world shifts around them. Over the years, I have gotten better at making trade decisions based on important news events, which translates into bigger wins and smaller losses. I have also found that once I purchase a stock, I am much more tuned into how it performs. As you watch the movements of stocks, you will learn a ton about how the larger financial markets work.

Second, I think it's important for new investors to make purchasing and selling decisions with liquid investments such as stocks. New investors need to attempt to know when to hold 'em and fold 'em. Learning that with stocks is a great gateway into less liquid and more expensive assets such as real estate.

Third, it's far easier to diversify with stocks than in real estate. With fractional share investing you can purchase very small dollar amounts of stock in as many stocks as you want, spreading your risk over different securities, sectors, and individual companies.

POP-UP DEFINITION

Fractional share investing - a relatively new feature offered by most brokerages that allows investors to buy a fraction of a share of a company or to buy just a specific dollar amount of that company. For example, one share of Booking Holdings (BKNG) currently costs over $3,000. With fractional share investing, I can buy 0.3 shares for about $900.

Fourth, and most importantly, it's crucial for new investors to learn how to lose money. Obviously, I don't want you to lose a lot of money, and I don't want you to lose money very often. However, one of the biggest stumbling blocks for new investors is coming to grips with the idea of taking risks that could ultimately result in losing some money. If you ever hear an investor tell you they have never lost money, they are either lying or playing a foolish emotional game where they refuse to sell loser securities until they recover back to break even.

There is one kind of investor that never loses money: Ponzi scheme operators like Bernie Madoff. Bernie took billions of dollars from investors by convincing them he had cracked the code for always winning in stocks. However, the truth is, he pocketed the money and sent the investors fake stock trade reports that showed a steady profit. Bernie died in prison for his crimes.

All legitimate investors will lose money on occasion. The key to losing money is to learn from your mistakes on each loss. You just need to make enough good bets that your overall result is a net positive. Investing relatively small amounts of money in the stock market is a great way to learn from periodic losses. It's a lot less stressful to lose a few dollars on one of your stock picks than to lose money on your one-and-only rental property, for example.

BUILDING YOUR 50/40/10 LIFESTYLE

Now, let's build your 50/40/10 lifestyle budget. Everything I say from this point forward is assuming you have adopted the minimalist mindset to convert your clutter into cash and you've paid off your consumer debt. Your transportation is LOGIC based, and you've converted your expensive hobbies into an income-generating side hustle. Finally, your house hack is generating enough money to cover your housing costs!

If all of this is true for you, you are absolutely crushing it and beautifully set up to build serious wealth. If you're still in the process of hacking your lifestyle, keep working at it and start your 50/40/10 budget at whatever level you are at because in the world of investing, time is, quite literally, money. In other words, don't wait for conditions to be perfect to get started. **Spoiler alert: Conditions will never be perfect. The best time to plant a tree was ten years ago. The second best time to plant a tree is today.** So even if you aren't yet able to invest a full 40%

of your income, apply what percentage you do have and work like mad to get to the 40% as soon as you can.

The 50/40/10 concept is simple. Add up all of the net income that comes into your personal finances from all sources. Net income includes your net take-home pay from your paycheck, 100% of dividends and interest income, business profits, and net cash flow from your real estate.

For example, if your house hack is generating $2,000 and your mortgage, maintenance, and management expenses are $1,800, then your net cash flow from your house hack is $200. You will only count the $200 as income in your 50/40/10 formula. Likewise, if your side hustle business is generating $1,000 per month in revenue, but your expenses to generate that income are $600, then the amount you use in your 50/40/10 budget is the $400 profit. Finally, you've gotten into the groove of generating points and cash worth $400 from your credit card hack every month. Assuming your monthly salary is $4,500, all totaled up, your total family income is $5,500. Here is your 50/40/10 budget income allocation:

- 50% for living expenses = $2,750
- 40% for investing = $2,200
- 10% for charitable giving = $550

While your 50% spending budget is only $2,750, it's important to look at the whole picture. When you were able to spend your entire $4,500 salary, you also had many more expenses that you eliminated after mastering the lifestyle hacks in the previous section. Here is a side-by-side comparison of someone with a $4,500 salary on the traditional model versus the HACKER method:

	Traditional Earn & Spend Method	HACKER Method	
Salary	$4,500.00	$4,500.00	
House Hack Cash Flow	$0.00	$200.00	
Side Hustle	$0.00	$400.00	
Credit Card Points Value	$0.00	$400.00	
Total Income	$4,500.00	$5,500.00	
Spending Portion %	100%	50%	
Spending Budget	$4,500.00	$2,750.00	
Expenses			
Mortgage/Rent & Utilities	$1,500.00	$500.00	← Reduced by your house hack
Vehicle Expenses	$1,000.00	$400.00	← Reduced by owning LOGIC vehicles
Groceries & dining	$900.00	$1,000.00	← Increased to **EAT BETTER**
Payroll Taxes	$350.00	$350.00	← Same
Vacation & Other	$200.00	$50.00	← Reduced through credit card point printing
Clothing/Personal Care	$200.00	$225.00	← Increased to **DRESS BETTER**
Revolving Debt Interest	$150.00	$0.00	← Paid off from estate sale
Entertainment	$100.00	$125.00	← Increased to **RELAX BETTER**
Out of pocket medical	$100.00	$100.00	←Same
Total Expenses	$4,500.00	$2,750.00	
Investing Portion	0%	40%	
Investing Budget	$0.00	$2,200	
Giving Portion	0%	10%	
Giving Budget	$0.00	$550	

In this scenario, the HACKER method has not only carved out a large amount for investing for the future and making the world a better place, we've also improved our standard of living in almost all the categories.

Now, let's have some fun calculating three scenarios to see what a $2,200/month investment will do for you in the long term.

Scenario #1 - $2,200 monthly investment contribution w/ no increases at 9.7% ROI

A simple FV (future value) formula in a spreadsheet will tell you that if you invest $2,200 every month over the course of 20 years, and if you get the same average ROI as the stock market over the last 90 years (9.7%), your investment account will grow to almost $1,500,000.

The best news, however, is that this is not the 50/40/10 model. The 50/40/10 model is designed to adjust to your constantly increasing income every year, which increases your 40% contribution to investing as well. In other words, your 40% allocated to investing will start at $2,200 but rise every year after that.

Scenario #2 - $2,200 monthly investment, 10% yearly income increases & seed funds at 9.7% ROI

Expanding from scenario #1, your 40% investment contribution is still $2,200 to start but now includes two new variables. First, let's assume you can kick off your investing fund with $20,000 that you generated from your estate sale, debt liquidation and asset sales in the HACKER step H. Second, we are going to add in an annual increase in your household income of 10%. Your salary doesn't have to increase 10% every year, but your lifestyle hacks and investments should contribute at least that every year. After we add these two variables into the formula, even keeping the 9.7% ROI and sticking with a twenty year timeline, your investment fund skyrockets to over $3,500,000! You'll cross the millionaire mark in just twelve years.

Scenario #3 - $2,200 monthly investment contribution w/ 10% annual increases at 15% ROI for 25 years

If you think that's amazing, watch this. While $3,500,000 is by no means a small number, it could grow much larger than that if you are able to beat the stock market's 9.7% average return and if you can add more time to the 50/40/10 process. Nothing is guaranteed in investing, but my real estate investing has generated closer to 15% annual returns, even after accounting for the devastating years of 2007 to 2013 when my real estate portfolio lost 40% of its value. If we stick with scenario #2, but we change the annual average return to 15% and increase the time from just under 20 years to 25, your investment portfolio would be worth more than $12,800,000! Today, that puts you in the wealthiest 1% of people on earth.

Okay, let's fast forward to 20 years from now and, just for simplicity's sake, use scenario #2 and assume you have accumulated a net worth of roughly $3,500,000. Imagine you shift gears from aggressive investor mode to a more steady and safe "retirement" mode. We can set your investment strategy to target only 5% ROI on your $3,500,000. In this case, your annual income from investments will be $179,000 per year without touching your $3.5 million fortune. You can be sleeping, sipping a cold drink in a hammock on the beach in Hawaii, running a marathon, volunteering at your favorite charity event, or hanging out with your family while $179,000 is dumped into your checking account every year.

I hope you see this like I do—as very exciting news! However, I can imagine that someone may look at this and be discouraged that it's going to take years to become a reality. If that's you, take a moment to think of a get-rich-quick scheme that actually made someone rich. I can't think of any, either. Even those unicorns who win the lottery usually end up broke not too long after winning.

One study reported by creditdonkey.com claims that 70% of Florida lottery winners were broke five years after winning. The reason for that, in my opinion, is they didn't have the skills to manage their instant wealth. Following the 50/40/10 lifestyle ensures you are less likely to fall into the same fate because you will be learning how to be financially astute along the way. Also, realize that I am using scenarios for a person living on a relatively low income. If your 40% is more than $2,200 every month, your numbers could be much higher, and your goals could come to fruition years earlier!

SETTING UP A BUDGET THAT WORKS IN THE REAL WORLD

Using the example above, create your own earn-and-spend report based on your actual current spending averages, and then reconstruct a new 50/40/10 budget. I want to stress that you need the gifts, vacation, entertainment, and other categories in your budget. The 50/40/10 budget is a marathon, not a sprint. You have to build a budget that gives you enough breathing room to enjoy life, even if that enjoyment is on the cheap at first. The worst thing to do is to allocate all of your funds to just paying the basic bills and eliminating all frills. You might be able to make it a year or two, but you'll abandon the whole concept sooner rather than later.

I understand that it's hard to limit spending, especially when on a tight income. The solution to that may be to make more money. I do not intend to state the obvious in a smug way. Rather, I want to inspire you to stop thinking with limited vision regarding your income. It has been said that you are making what you think you deserve to make and not a penny more or a penny less. Even just starting a side hustle as advised in Hacking Your Lifestyle is a great way to boost income.

I made the choice to work in the non-profit sector, and the expectation by pretty much everyone was that I was not allowed to make a huge salary. In the very beginning, I didn't make very much. But I decided to focus more on building up a base of donors to increase my income, and with the exception of one year, my personal income increased every year. It meant doing a lot of intentional work, but I did what it took to increase it to better provide for my family and to keep my investments growing. I encourage you to do the same.

Assuming you are ready to start your 50/40/10 budget, you need a vital tool to ensure you stay on track for the long term. It's nearly impossible to stay on track if you only casually glance at your bills or even if you reconcile your accounts monthly, and just too easy to spend over budget if you're not keeping track of expenses daily.

My wife and I have personal spending tracking apps on our phones that we have been using for over ten years. There are dozens of them out there. They are incredibly helpful for tracking how much you've spent in each category, each month. We've also found they are a great tool to help reconcile the bank and credit card statements each month. If you can't find an app that works for you, you can use a simple spreadsheet or even an old-fashioned notepad and pen. Whatever the method, find a way to track your spending and make a commitment as a family to track every purchase.

As we close out this section on the practical application of 50/40/10, we need to address the elephant in the room and the temptation to chip away at the 10% charitable giving category. This may be the category that is most tempting to take from to make your spending or investing budgets work. Don't do it.

I go into more depth in chapter 21 on the ethics of building wealth. But the bottom line is, the 10% giving category is vital to your quest to build wealth. It may not help your return on investment. It probably doesn't boost your spending power. But it does something for your soul and your character that no amount of frugality or ROI can. Being charitable gives you the ability to leave the world a better place than you found it. Jesus is quoted as saying, "What good is it for a man to gain the whole world, yet forfeit their soul?" You don't have to be religious to know the answer to this question. None of us seek out to be a cartoonish cigar-chomping miser with a one-track goal to get rich at all costs, but if we fail to keep a portion of our wealth set aside for altruistic generosity and benevolence, we eventually could be mistaken for one.

HACKER SECTION 3

CASH
IS KING
INVESTING

CHAPTER 12

REPENT FROM YOUR RISK AVERSION

THE BIGGEST RISK IS NOT TAKING ANY.

Tumbleweeds blowing down the street outnumber buyers on this windy and warm morning in August 2009 in Meridian, Idaho. The sellers are huddled with the auction house manager as they nervously watch the clock tick down to the published auction start time. Aside from me and my wife, the only other buyers present are one couple and a single gentleman. The sellers are unable to hide their disappointment from the lack of turnout. They had hoped that the "no reserve price" they promoted would bring out hoards of buyers looking for a deal. The start time comes and goes but they stall, waiting for a few more buyers that never show up.

There are two tracts of land for sale. The first one is three adjacent townhome lots, and the second is four more adjacent townhome lots. The auctioneer starts the bidding on the three lots. All three buyers got in when the bidding was under $10,000 per lot. Once the price got over $10,000, the other couple bowed out, leaving just the single man and us in the hunt. As we bid each other up, my heart was pounding faster and faster. I had never before been at an auction where tens of thousands of dollars were at stake. It's hard to describe the conflicting emotions I was feeling as both fear and exhilaration gripped me at the same time. It felt like everything was running in slow motion as all of my senses were on high alert.

When the price got to $15,000 per lot, my nerves got the best of me, and I stopped bidding. I wanted those three lots, but I knew I didn't have enough money in my 40% investment account to buy both tracts of land, so I decided to fight for the next four lots over just these three. After I stopped bidding, the auctioneer's face went from a fearful yellow to a mad red. He walked up closely to me, stared directly into my eyes, and raised his voice— trying to get me to come back in. Even though my heart felt like it was going to leap out of my chest, I didn't cave. I hoped this other buyer would be happy with these three lots, removing my primary competition for the other four lots. Going once, twice, sold…the other buyer got the three lots for $15,000 each. The auctioneer's face betrayed his frustration, and my pulse began to come back to earth.

The whole group walked over to the four lots, and the process started again. Just as I had hoped, the buyer of the three lots never entered the bid for the four. The other couple only bid me up twice, and I got the four lots for $13,000 each. The seller, who had been completely silent thus far, somberly turned around, got in his truck, and drove off. The auctioneer shoved the pledge sheet over to me to sign. I later found out that the sellers had paid $80,000 for each of the seven lots in 2007, just before the greatest housing crash in 80 years!

This is not a unique story for 2009, the first full year of the Great Recession. That recession was sparked by fundamental weaknesses in the real estate market, which had been compounding for years. After the bubble burst in 2008, real estate in America had been in free fall, and many investors, builders, and realtors were losing their businesses. Many homeowners who lost their jobs lost their homes too, which flooded the market with properties at fire-sale prices. The lots that were auctioned that day were caught in the perfect storm. They were townhomes amidst single-family homes. They were bare lots amidst a fully built-out subdivision. Worst of all for the sellers, they were purchased on speculation before the bubble peaked and liquidated in a panic after it popped. Understandably, most investors who hadn't yet lost everything were terrified that values would continue to decline.

I hired a builder friend of mine to build the townhomes, and they were completed in late 2010. We got really good deals on materials and construction labor because the suppliers and trades were hungry for work and eager to negotiate. All in, we paid $107,000 for each 1,225-square-foot, three-bed/two-bath townhome. That's $87.35 per square foot, about 40% under the price of new construction at the height of the boom. Twelve years later, those homes appraised for $385,000 each. On the value side, our $428,000 project is now worth over $1.5 million. On the income side, our first tenants paid $850 rent per month. Today, these units are generating over $46,000 per year in positive cash flow as short-term rentals.

I wanted to share this story with you because I feel like it's a powerful way to paint the picture of the importance of taking measured risk. It is impossible to underplay how nervous I was during the auction. I had close personal friends who had already lost everything in that crash. Before 2008, I had never even heard of a short sale. By the time the auction happened, I knew many people who short-sold their homes, moved into small rental apartments, and were living in survival mode! In my non-profit work, I was surrounded by many wealthy business people who were laying off employees and taking a huge hit from the cratering economy. There was a sense that America was heading into an extremely severe recession, maybe even another depression.

Some experts were predicting that real estate would either never fully recover or take decades to come back. Shelling out $52,000 for four empty lots was a real risk. Credit markets were freezing up, and there was a real chance we would not get the funding to build those homes, or even worse, lose the funding mid-way through the project. Few people were predicting a strong rental market in the near term. In fact, most were predicting a softening or even a crash in rental rates to follow the crash in home values.

In spite of the cascade of daunting risks, we showed up at that auction hoping to expand our real estate portfolio at bargain prices, and that's exactly what we did. In all honesty, we had no idea those townhomes would perform so well, but we were pretty sure they would eventually go up in value and produce positive income for our family for a long time. My hope is that this story will enable you to make a significant mentality shift from that of most people. While humans are the most intelligent beings on earth, we are still very emotion-driven and prone to making irrational decisions based on too much fear.

DON'T BE A CAVE DWELLER

Our cave-dwelling ancestors developed survival skills to protect themselves against other human attackers and hungry bears. They learned to be paranoid of the sound of every snapping twig in the forest, and they huddled together in tight-knit family clans because there was safety in numbers. That instinct is still deeply embedded in our brains today. I often make an analogy of humans with birds. There could be 1,000 sparrows all flying in one direction. All it takes is a horn honk to get all 1,000 birds to stop in mid-flight and turn away from the scary sound. You can watch this dynamic play out with highly intelligent humans every day in the stock market. One day the markets are up 3% on some supposedly coded message from the chairman of the federal reserve. The next day the market could crater 2% because Boeing missed its quarterly earnings consensus by a few cents. Nothing in the world economy materially changed on either day. There was a loud, scary sound, and investors—millions of very smart investors—stopped mid-flight and changed course, all based on an emotional response to fear.

In his 1933 inauguration, at the darkest economic time of the last 100 years, FDR famously said, "The only thing we have to fear is fear itself." Things had gotten so bad during the Great Depression that people were hiding money under their mattresses or behind the plaster in their walls, and burying gold and silver in tin cans in their backyard. Roosevelt realized the only thing holding the mighty American economy back was money stashed in hiding and not circulating in the economy. Collective fear had a firm grip on everything. FDR knew we had technology, factories, farms, banks, an educated and growing population, and a decent infrastructure. In his view, there was no inherent reason why the Depression had to continue. The fundamentals of America were sound. While there are always threats and weaknesses in any nation and in any economy, there is sufficient reason to believe that America today is even stronger than it was 100 years ago.

Bill Gates and Warren Buffett, two of the wealthiest people on earth, were interviewed at the height of the economic turmoil of the Great Recession, and they both expressed optimism for the future of the American economy. They agreed that America is still the invention leader of the world and still able to innovate in ways most nations cannot. In a 2018 interview with CNN, Warren Buffett was asked if he felt that the nine-year strong economic run was going to stall. He said, "America has been on a 242-year economic run; I mean, it just gets interrupted a little bit, but there was nothing here in 1776 and look at what we've done! … I'm not worried about the long-term future of America, and I don't worry about the short-term, either."

Cave dwellers were justified in retreating at the slightest sound of danger because their lives and the lives of their families were literally at risk every day. Unfortunately, we seem to react to financial risk as if our very lives were at risk. Your life can fundamentally change for the good if you can look at money for what it is and stop looking at it for what it is not. Money is 1) a store of value, 2) a simplified bartering instrument, and 3) a unit of labor. Money is not 1) your future, 2) your beating heart, or 3) your very life. If you lose money, you will still have a future, your heart will still be beating, and you'll still be alive. If you are willing to allow yourself to pull money off the pedestal, your views on putting it at risk might change for the better.

Throughout the process of buying those townhome lots, we felt all of the cave-dweller danger emotions. Our instincts were yelling at us to hide our cash in a can and RUN! To be honest, those instincts were not completely off in the short term because Idaho real estate continued to lose value until 2012. Those four townhomes actually went down in value before they went up. But those primitive instincts were completely wrong for the long term. **In order for you to be a successful investor of any kind and build real wealth, you must first learn how to handle your fear, then make a calculated assessment of the most likely future outcome, and make a bold move. You need to learn to hear the scary sounds, assess the long-term risk and reward, and act with confidence.**

I have talked with many people who have told me they were sick of their jobs and wanted to get into real estate or some other passive investment vehicle to find financial freedom. Very few of them get started, and my hunch is that it's mostly based on the cave-dwelling fear instinct that is so strong in us all. Don't let the cave-dweller fear control you. Don't confuse money with your life. Don't stay stuck at a job where your earning potential and future economic outlook are capped. Stop cowering in fear at the scary sounds you hear every time you take a peek at creating a better economic future for your family. Stop looking at money as something you have to have a death grip on in order to keep it. The only way to grow wealth is to release your grip and send your money out into the world to go to work.

It might shock you to know that even the most experienced investors regularly battle with cave-dweller fear. I certainly do. Every time I make an investment, whether it's for a $3 million condo development or a stock purchase for a few hundred dollars, I feel that primitive fear. The moment before I release the death grip on my cash, I always feel at least a little bit uneasy about it. My mind races with the what-if scenarios. I worry about the money leaving and never coming back. I worry about looking stupid in front of my friends. Over time, however, I have learned to handle and even use the inner cave dweller instincts as I analyze potential investments, which leads me to the skill of assessing the risks of investing, otherwise known as "due diligence."

SOBERLY ASSESSING RISK

While I do want you to release your grip on your cash and start investing, I don't suggest you do so blindly, based on hope alone. Rather, you need to create a process to assess each investment. I have made hundreds, maybe thousands, of individual investments in my life and have developed a process that helps me make wise investments. My process has only three simple steps and works for investments of any size or type.

First, I identify what my goal is. Any investment I make must be tied to what I am trying to accomplish. Second, I make a thorough analysis of the investment to assess its potential upside, downside, and timeline to sell the asset to bank profits. I always use conservative growth estimates and liberal cost or risk estimates. I want to see if the investment will perform even if things don't go perfectly (because they won't!). Finally, I run through "what if" scenarios. You might even say—I let the cave dweller in to tell me why I shouldn't do the deal. The important thing here is, the cave dweller doesn't have all the say. The first two steps in the process have equal or more say. The cave dweller might have some valid points that can make me take a closer look and tighten down my risk mitigation plan.

I also don't let the cave dweller come up with possible but ridiculous scenarios. The cave dweller always talks about nuclear attacks, 10.0 earthquakes, and bus-sized meteor strikes. Those are always discarded because if one of those happens, the last thing we're worried about is our balance sheet. The cave dweller can also come up with other possibilities that also need to be ignored. For example, during the townhome lot auction, the cave dweller was telling me that the recession was going to become a depression and I was going to lose everything. Technically, that was possible. Some smart people were predicting just that at the time. However, when this is the only scenario where my investment falls apart, I almost always proceed anyway for two reasons. First, there's only been one depression in the last 150 years in America, so they are extremely rare, and the odds are in my favor it won't happen again in my lifetime. Second, if we go into a deep depression, everyone is going to lose everything, so at least I'll be in good company. I refuse to stay on the sidelines and watch opportunities pass me by because of extremely unlikely risk events. Besides, my skills as an investor will enable me to recover, and hopefully I learn a couple of things in the process.

UNDERSTANDING "RISK" VOCABULARY

I want to conclude this chapter by addressing a vocabulary problem surrounding the word "risk." If you ask Google, the first definition of risk that pops up is "noun; a situation involving exposure to danger." A few of Google's synonyms of risk are "danger," "peril," and "threat." If this is the definition most people think of when hearing the word risk, it's no wonder we get a little freaked out about "risking" money.

Using Google's definition of risk, the first thing that comes to my mind is wingsuit jumping, also called wingsuiting. Wingsuiting has been dubbed by some as the deadliest sport on earth. A wingsuit is just what it sounds like: It's a suit that a person can put on that has nylon wings under the arms and between the legs. People put these wingsuits on, jump off cliffs, and "fly" like a glider. After the initial free fall, the wind catches under the wings, and the jumper flies forward three feet for every foot they drop at the speed of 100 miles per hour. Sounds risky, right? It is! Roughly one in twenty wingsuiters die doing their sport. Even professionals who pour thousands of hours into their sport are at a serious risk of danger on every jump.

Our job as investors is to learn how to differentiate between wingsuit types of financial risk where the odds are dangerously not in our favor and a more calculated risk where the odds actually are strongly in our favor. While no investment is risk-free, with time, you should learn to not only tolerate risk, but look for ways to "risk" your money in a measured way that will likely create good returns.

I am not saying there's no financial investment parallel to wingsuiting. Most casino gambling has loss odds similar to or even worse than wingsuiting. There are also fraudsters out there peddling false investments. Additionally, making investments without proper training, experience, and mentorship could cause you to lose money. Finally, investing money that is needed to provide the basic family needs is also a very risky venture to avoid. I do not advocate gambling, investing without thorough due diligence, or investing funds you need to live on.

POP-UP DEFINITION

Due diligence - the process of completely investigating the validity of an investment's calculations, claims, assumptions and projections.

If you follow every single tip, trick, and hack in this book, but don't learn to take carefully calculated risks with your money, you will not become wealthy. In other words, the path to building significant wealth is to put your money at risk in investments that have an acceptable risk versus reward ratio. I cannot tell you what that ratio is for you. Only you can decide what that ratio is. When you first start out, you'll probably begin with less risky and, therefore, less lucrative investments. There is nothing wrong with that, by the way. As you gain experience and develop investing instincts, you'll graduate to investment vehicles that tend to carry more risk but generate higher returns.

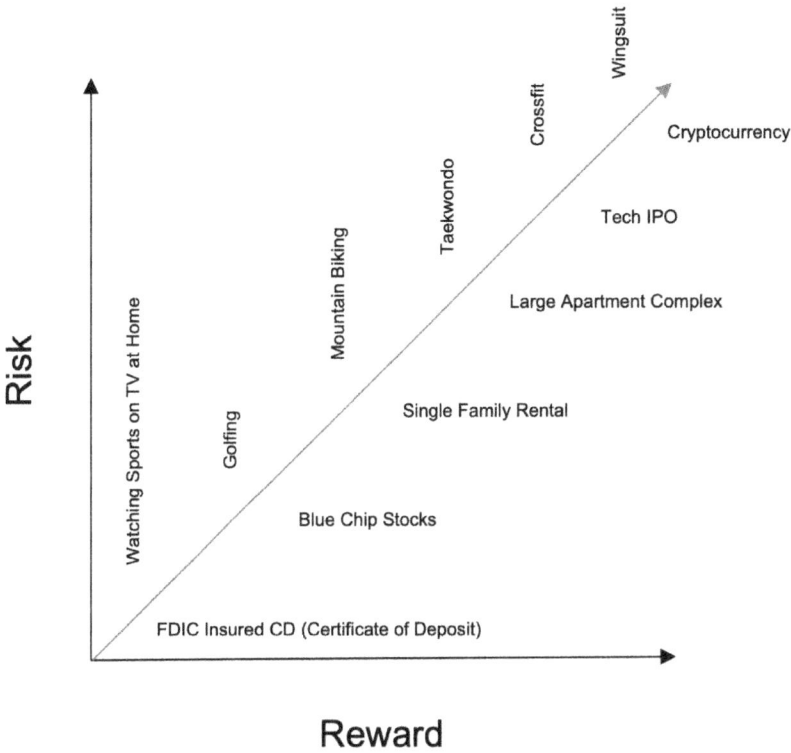

I created a chart above that visually illustrates the risk versus reward calculus. The items on the right side of the red arrow are commonly known and understood asset classes that people can invest in with the hope of generating a return on their investment. The items on the left side of the arrow are sporting activities that can create an adrenaline rush. Please don't get hung up on the placement of any sport or asset class on the chart. It's merely an overly simplified illustration to help you visualize the calculus of risk versus reward.

Let's take the risk versus reward ratio of watching a sporting event on TV at home. Watching our favorite team on TV can give us a rush.

When we score, we get a true shot of adrenaline. However, that shot is minimal, and the sensation is short-lived when you compare it to the rush we feel as actual players in a game. Therefore, the reward of watching TV exists, but is minimal. On the risk side of the equation, watching TV at home carries very minimal cost or risk. Pretty much the only way to get injured watching sports on TV is by choking on a pretzel as we leap in the air after our team scores.

Now let's look at the risk versus reward ratio of the counterpart to watching sports on TV, which is investing in a federally insured certificate of deposit (CD). As of this writing, my bank is offering a 4.35% annual interest rate on CDs. In other words, for every $100 in my CD account for an entire year, I get $4.35 in interest. With inflation raging at over 6%, the CD isn't even keeping up with rising prices. So, there is a reward from this investment, but the reward is minimal. On the risk side of the equation, there's very little risk because CDs in American banks are guaranteed by the U.S. government up to $250,000. The only risk would be for the U.S. economy to implode and subsequently for the U.S. government to go into default. Possible, but not very likely. So investing in CDs is very low risk, but very low return as well.

As you climb the risk versus reward ladder, there is more opportunity for adrenaline rushes in sports and financial returns in investing. As the adrenaline rush in sports increases, so do the risks of injury. The same is true in investing. As you invest in assets that have potential increased returns on investment, the risks of losing money also increase with it. However, there are ways to mitigate your risks in both sports and investing. In Tae Kwon Do, for example, nobody starts out as a black belt. Everyone starts with a white belt and has to earn their way up the belt ladder by mastering certain skills and disciplines. However, investing in the financial world isn't as organized as the belt system in

Tae Kwon Do. The onus is on the investor to study each asset class they want to invest in and ensure they have the skills to perform the due diligence needed to invest confidently.

When we first start out, the risks we face on any investment are higher than when we are more experienced. As with anything in life, there's a learning curve. The good news is, however, as you gain experience, confidence, and skill, you can actually push down the riskiness of your investments and even boost your reward. Common sense says that someone who has purchased 100 single-family home rentals is much more likely to make a smarter purchase than someone purchasing their first one.

In the next chapter, we are going to attempt to peek into the minds of millionaire investors and see what separates them from most people. As we do this, I want you to start thinking about finding a mentor who has already reached the level of success you want. Lean on that mentor to help you assess risks and perform due diligence before you invest. This mentor will help you avoid costly mistakes and embolden you to take action at the same time. In my opinion, there's no replacement for a wise mentor in the world of investing. You might also be surprised at how willing accomplished people are to help new up-and-comers like you. Don't be afraid to reach out!

CHAPTER 13

THE UPSIDE DOWN MIND OF A MILLIONAIRE

WEALTHY PEOPLE BUY LUXURIES LAST.

In the Netflix series Stranger Things, the characters interact with a place they call the Upside Down. The Upside Down is essentially an alternate universe from reality. It has the same basic geographic locations, buildings, etc., but it's just completely opposite of reality. If reality is light, the upside down is dark. If reality is hot, the upside down is cold. If reality is predictable, the upside down is chaotic.

Netflix made the Upside Down an evil and dangerous place. I am not saying people with a wealth-building mindset are evil and dangerous. What I am saying is that it's not uncommon for people who are not wealthy to look into the alternate universe of the wealthy and interpret evil things. While I reject the conventional wisdom and media hype that wealthy people are the cause of all that's wrong with the world, I do acknowledge that wealthy people live in an alternate universe from most people living in the lower classes. Wealthy people think and act in a way that seems upside down from how most "normal" people live.

In order to build wealth, you must first learn the upside-down thinking of wealthy people, then start to live in the upside-down world that wealthy people live in. However, it's important to not only mimic the things wealthy people do, but also to grasp a new, healthier view of the upside-down ways of the wealthy. You cannot both emulate the actions and decisions of the wealthy and harbor resentment or suspicion of wealthy people in general at the same time. Doing so would cause you to feel like you are literally trying to survive the Stranger Things version of the Upside Down.

As you read through the rest of this chapter, attempt to put yourself in the shoes of a real-life human being who happens to be a wealthy investor. Realize that you love your family, feel a deep sense of duty to serve your community, and have a genuine desire to make a positive impact on the world with your wealth. I know hundreds of millionaires and have yet to meet one that embodies the character of Mr. Burns from The Simpsons. Some of the gentlest, most generous, and most caring people I know have tens of millions of dollars to their name. Reject the media's demonization of rich people, and open your mind to learning new ways to see wealth building and the people who master the craft.

UPSIDE DOWN MINDSET #1: MILLIONAIRES LIVE CHEAP

People with a wealth-building mindset operate the opposite of most people in the realm of spending. Most wealthy people live frugally, or at least they start out that way. I know a lady with a net worth of over $6 million who still hunts for coupons to go grocery shopping. Warren Buffett still lives in the house he bought in 1958, well before he was a billionaire. To people with a wealth-building mindset, this is a natural response to the understanding of how money works. The more we spend when we don't have any money, the harder it is to acquire wealth. We understand that the only way to build real wealth is to invest as much of our discretionary income as possible. This mindset drives us to spend money sparingly, often even after we have achieved success.

UPSIDE DOWN MINDSET #2: MILLIONAIRES WORK HARD TO ADD DEBT

Wealthy people almost all use debt as leverage to accelerate their wealth building. It's almost comical to listen to wealthy people talk about debt. I have sat through entire meals arguing about the best way to collateralize millions in debt, how to squeeze the lender for another 0.125%, and which loan terms are negotiable, etc. Investors talk exhaustively about debt instruments like car enthusiasts talk about engines.

I do know a few older guys who still operate in a "cash only" mentality. However, especially in the real estate investment world, debt is almost universally accepted as an essential tool to wealth expansion. Responsible and conservative borrowing against stable income-producing assets is a powerful wealth builder, and wealthy people have no problem bringing on this kind of debt. See the chapter on the five boosters of real estate investing for a deeper dive into this subject.

UPSIDE DOWN MINDSET #3: MILLIONAIRES KNOW CASH IS CRAP

Charlie Rose was interviewing Warren Buffett in 2012, and in a discussion about his philosophy on cash, Warren snarkily remarked, "Cash is crap!" That's an interesting comment from a guy who routinely has over $100,000,000,000 (that's 100 billion) in cash on his company's balance sheet. The reason why Buffett so flippantly made that comment stems from his orientation around money, investing, and all things financial.

The reason why cash truly is crap is because inflation is constantly eroding the value of any currency. This is why it's somewhere between hard and impossible for "savers" to build serious wealth. A less exciting but more informative way to say "Cash is crap" would be to say, "Pile your cash into income-producing assets that appreciate." Had Buffett said that mouthful, nobody would have ever quoted him though. Nonetheless, that's the topic of this chapter. The millionaire sees money (or cash) in a very different way from people stuck in the lower economic classes.

Before I had even heard Buffett's "cash is crap" sound bite, I had been known to say, "I hate cash!" I have to admit, like Buffett, I have said that on occasion just to get a reaction out of people. But the sentiment accurately reflects my general attitude toward holding large amounts of cash. Any time I have an exit event or some other reason to have more than $100,000 in a bank account, I catch myself getting anxious. I've even gotten short-tempered with my family because of it.

I once had $625,000 wired to my account from the sale of some land. After the wire was confirmed, I went berserk! I got really agitated and fidgety. I went through the whole house and rearranged all the closets and drawers and cleaned everyone's room, putting stuff where I thought it should go. I reorganized all the bookshelves, then cleaned out the garage and was still looking for things to "fix." I didn't consciously know it, but I was a mix of mad, scared, and nervous that I had a bunch of cash sitting there. So, my brain found other things that needed to be "fixed" as a way to cope with the stress of sitting on a lot of cash. Within a week, I found ways to reinvest that cash, and I calmed right back down. My nervous system subconsciously reacted this way for four reasons.

First, I have a healthy distrust of banks in general and more than a little paranoia about identity theft. Why should I trust title companies, mortgage brokerages, or other people who know about a six-figure deposit that just hit my account? They have my social security number, date of birth, my signature, and sometimes my bank account number on a wire form—it's a recipe for fraud and theft!

Second, I know that cash loses value at the rate of inflation. A day or a week doesn't have much of an impact, but a month does. A year really does!

Third, the worst part of having cash in the bank is that it's not generating a return from an investment. Just using simple math, a 10% return on $100,000 will generate $10,000 in profits in a year. Currently, I only consider investments that project to return at least 20% annually. Assuming we can get a 20% return on our cash, $100,000 left in the bank for just ninety days will cause you to lose out on $5,000 in gains!

Fourth, the only thing worse than holding excessive cash that isn't generating a return is the risk of spending the cash on unnecessary luxuries. Even for the most disciplined among us (me included), piles of available cash can start to whisper in our ears about all the things we deserve to buy. The longer cash sits there, the more those whispers turn into shouts.

The most efficient and prudent use of cash is to hold only enough to protect against unknown future challenges and to cover normal operating expenses. This doesn't just apply to a business you might run, but to your personal finances as well. Most people from a middle-class background think that rich people have lots of cash in the bank. In fact, I've heard wealthy people say things like, "I have ten million dollars in the bank." That's almost certainly not true. It's just a phrase they say, but what they mean is they have ten million dollars in net worth. Usually, a small percentage of that is held in actual cash in an actual bank.

Now, you might be saying, I don't have $100,000 in the bank, so I don't have that problem. Most people don't start out with $100,000 to invest. But the people who learn cash is crap will constantly do things that will turn $1,000 into $2,000, then $10,000, then $100,000 through releasing cash from the bank and into investments that grow.

UPSIDE DOWN MINDSET #4: MILLIONAIRES BUY ASSETS & SELL TOYS

The most important thing wealthy people do that most ordinary folks do not is they buy assets that have the potential to generate an income and increase in value over time. Most people wouldn't even know what an income-producing asset is. One time, I gave a key employee a $10,000 bonus that they weren't expecting. They were obviously really thankful and even got a little emotional. After the shock wore off, they asked me genuinely what they should do with it. Without even thinking, I said, "Buy income-producing assets!" They looked at me as if I was speaking Chinese and asked, "How do I do that?" I suggested buying a small fixer-upper rental property or buying stocks. My advice was met with a muttered comment about the coming recession. I'm pretty sure the $10,000 went into savings.

When I say wealthy people sell toys, I'm actually referring to two concepts, neither of which is only about "toys," per se. As we discussed in the first HACKER section "Hack Your Lifestyle," people with a millionaire mind are special when it comes to buying fancy toys. One of my favorite wealth-building zingers is, "Poor people buy luxuries first. Wealthy people buy luxuries last." Tied in with the idea of living cheaply, many wealthy people have a high level of discipline when buying expensive toys like sports cars, boats, TVs, and other electronics. High-dollar toys that aren't necessary to live a comfortable life steal money from our investment activities, so they avoid doing it.

Not only do wealthy people avoid buying expensive toys at the expense of investing, we are the ones who sell those same toys to the masses for a profit. While I was living overseas, I bought and sold dozens of homes, but was renting a small apartment to live in. Even today, I don't have a pool at my personal residence, but I own several homes with pools. Rather than dump $70,000 into a pool for myself, I'd rather boost the rent I can collect at a home that has a pool. That's the mindset of an investor.

UPSIDE DOWN MINDSET #5: MILLIONAIRES MAKE THE METER RUN BACKWARDS

A couple of years ago, I had a tax problem. My real estate was performing so well that I was facing a tax bill in spite of depreciation write-offs my real estate holdings usually provide. So, I started hunting for legal ways to slash my taxes. The U.S. government was offering a 26% credit for solar install costs, so I ran the numbers. One of my rental houses had a perfectly sloped roof for solar, which kept the system cost low. After accounting for the tax credit and the power bill savings, I calculated that I'd get my initial solar investment back in five years! That's a 20% annual ROI, so I pulled the trigger.

As soon as the system was installed, I went out to the property and found the power meter. It was still slowly spinning in the normal direction. I yelled at my handyman to shut off the AC. The meter slowed to a stop, hesitated for a few seconds, then actually started to run backwards! I felt like a kid in a candy store! My solar panels were pushing power back to the power company, and I was racking up credits in my Idaho Power account.

While solar itself is not always great from a pure ROI perspective, getting the meter to run backwards is a concept I want to implant in your mind. The millionaire mind is constantly trying to reverse the natural flow of money. The natural flow of money for most people is OUT of our account. From the day we move out of our parents' house and become responsible for our own living expenses, there's an almost frantic push to get a job so we can pay the rent, buy groceries, make the car payment, etc. Maybe we get raises or promoted to better jobs, but our expenses always seem to consume our entire paycheck or more! If we're not careful, we can rack up revolving credit card debt just to keep up with our lifestyle that our salary can no longer support.

Wealthy people install systems in their lives that reverse the natural outward flow of money. We put a limit on spending and force ourselves to invest in assets that actually put money into our accounts. We don't increase our spending until the flow of money back into our accounts is large enough to sustain it. Eventually, the flow of money back into our accounts is so strong, we don't need a salary from a job, so we quit. We then live on the backflow of money from our investments and use our new-found time gained from not working a 9-5 job to get even more effective at investing. That, in turn, has the tendency to push even more back into our wealth creation system.

Let's dive a bit deeper into the lives of a typical middle-class household using the electrical meter analogy. Let's say that the power flowing into the house is our salary. The money we make at our jobs is funding the operations of our house. Our income determines how much power we can consume. Now let's look at the things we buy as if they were appliances that consume the power created by our salary. Our car payment, Netflix subscription, and mortgage payments all plug into the power source and draw funds from it. In this scenario, the cycle is neverending. To keep all of the appliances plugged in, we must keep generating a salary, which requires us to work. If we have too many appliances plugged in, we have to take a second job or get loans to keep the lights on. Worst of all, pulling too much juice from the system can cause us to trip a breaker, and we have a nervous breakdown!

People with the millionaire mind, however, do two fundamental things differently. First, we habitually consume less power than what is available, and second, we buy investments that feed money back into the bank accounts, like a solar panel feeds power into the grid. When those investments start producing a lot more power, rather than plugging in more appliances to use up that power, we take the profits and buy more solar panels, ramping up the available power even more. We keep this cycle up until our meter starts to run backwards and we can stop working for a paycheck.

Rather than looking at wealthy people as if they are evil because they don't behave the way most people behave, study what they do and ask yourself why they do what they do. Then compare what they do to what you do and learn the reasons why the most successful people on earth seemingly live upside-down lives in an upside-down reality!

CHAPTER 14

QUINTUPLE POWER OF REAL ESTATE INVESTING

REAL ESTATE IS WHERE FOUNDATIONS FIND BEDROCK AND DREAMS FIND SKY.

Almost everyone has at least heard of Andrew Carnegie. Most of us know that he was one of the men who led America's industrial revolution through the creation of the Carnegie Steel Company. A few of us may have heard that he sold his company to J.P. Morgan in 1901 for $480,000,000 (worth about $16 billion today, adjusting for inflation). However, I would guess none of us would have attributed the following quote to Mr. Carnegie: "Ninety percent of all millionaires become so through owning real estate. More money has been made in real estate than in all industrial investments combined. The wise young man or wage earner of today invests his money in real estate" [emphasis mine]. Realize that when Carnegie said this, someone who could claim millionaire status in his time would have to have over $30,000,000 today.

It seems disingenuous to me that he would say such a thing. Think about it; Carnegie made his vast fortune in steel, not real estate. Why would he not say that millionaires are born through cornering commodities like steel or through creating union-busting monopolies? Unfortunately, we don't have a record as to why he made such a claim, so the best we can do is read between the lines and guess.

My theory is that Carnegie knew he was uniquely positioned physically in the United States in general and in Pennsylvania specifically. He was uniquely talented in managing markets and arranging people. He was also uniquely situated in history right at the upswing of the Industrial Revolution to catch the wave of American steel development.

Of course, Carnegie worked hard and was brilliant. But if I can boil his real estate claim down to the simplest explanation, Carnegie knew that he got extremely lucky to build such unbelievable wealth through steel. His bold claim about real estate being a superior investment to steel essentially takes the luck of his personal situation out of the equation. He knew that there was only ever going to be one Carnegie Steel, just like there is only one Google today. Carnegie Steel was not replicable, and its success was impossible without the perfect timing he enjoyed. Real estate, however, is the most timeless wealth builder the world has ever known and is available to anyone with the guts to step up to the plate, and he knew it.

If you're like me, you love to be inspired by people like Andrew Carnegie. In all honesty, however, there's a voice deep down in my mind that has a hard time relating to people like Carnegie or other financial giants like Bill Gates or Elon Musk. They are truly special people who possess almost supernatural business acumen. Sometimes I catch myself thinking, "Maybe for him, but I'm not him. I don't think I can get things to work for me like he can." We could read Carnegie's words and come up with many reasons why his perspective was unique to him, to his time, or to an economic environment that has long faded from reality. However, history is riddled with other people, even people not known to be business savvy, who have made similar claims about investing in real estate.

Mark Twain famously said, "Buy land. They're not making it any more." Will Rogers also quipped, "Don't wait to buy real estate. Buy real estate and wait." President Franklin D. Roosevelt blessed us with his wisdom when he said, "Real estate cannot be lost or stolen, nor can it be carried away. Purchased with common sense, paid for in full, and managed with reasonable care, it is about the safest investment in the world."

Standing humbly amidst these incredibly influential people, I have also accepted the fact that the surest path to true wealth is through the careful, methodical, conservative investment in real property. Almost all the wealthy people I know own real estate. Some of them got wealthy from real estate investing directly. Most of the rest have taken a portion of their salaries or business profits and poured it into real estate. For the latter, it's almost as if they felt a little bit like Carnegie. So what is it about real estate that is almost universally seen as a lucrative wealth builder?

To understand the power of real estate investing, let's look at the term "real estate" itself. Why don't we just refer to it as "property" or "land?" If you think about it, the words "real estate" don't really make sense in modern English. According to fastexpert.com, the term "real estate" was first recorded in 1660 in England as the title given to a king's grant of land. The word "real" comes from the Latin word "realis," meaning existing, actual, or genuine. The root word for estate is the old French word "estat," meaning status. So, real estate essentially means "genuine status" or "actual status." As cringeworthy as this divisive language sounds to us today, we must remember that the primary thing that separated the ruling class from peasants throughout all of civilized history is land ownership. Even in the United States, only landowners were allowed to vote until laws began to change in the 1820s. Let's now shift from looking at the history of real estate and look to the stars as an analogy for wealth building through real estate.

FINANCIAL ESCAPE VELOCITY

As a kid who grew up in the '80s and '90s, I have fond memories of watching the space shuttle blast off into space. The power, speed, and majesty of the entire process, from the countdown to launch to arrival in space, was awe-inspiring. The massive white clouds and 100-foot-long flames that shot out from under the engines at liftoff captured the attention of little boys and represented the ultimate human accomplishment to me. The almost unimaginable power created to launch a rocket is absolutely essential in order for humans to hope to escape Earth's gravitational pull and reach outer space.

Escape velocity is the term used to describe that moment when an object has reached a distance far enough away from Earth and at a speed fast enough to be no longer pulled immediately back to the surface by gravity. Once an object reaches escape velocity, the power required to remain in space is dramatically reduced and, eventually, eliminated completely.

Building lasting wealth is similar to the process of launching a rocket into space. It takes careful planning, precise execution, and course corrections along the way. But most of all, it takes a lot of channeled energy to go from a standstill on the ground to climbing so high you escape the grip of financial gravity.

Financial gravity is an invisible force that affects everyone. The lower a person is on the economic ladder, the more powerful the force of financial gravity that acts on that person. For those living meal to meal or even paycheck to paycheck, it can feel as though no amount of effort will ever lift us off the ground and out of the rat race. Anyone who has skipped a meal the day rent is due painfully understands what I'm talking about. The hours worked never seem to produce enough money to meet the basic needs to live a dignified life.

For those who have reached into the middle class or even upper middle class, we've gotten up off the ground a little and are no longer worried about our next meal, but we still live with the constant pressure of the mortgage payment, saving to pay for the kids' college, and planning for a livable retirement, all at the same time. Financial gravity is a bit weaker than it is for the lower classes, but it is still powerful enough to pull us back down at the slightest economic hiccup. A job loss, a massive medical bill, or something along those lines will push us right back down to earth.

Even people considered rich who make very large salaries are still bound by financial gravity. These people earn high incomes, but their lifestyle obligations and lack of income-producing assets force them to keep trading time for money to stay off the ground. The moment they let up, financial gravity will bring them back to earth. So, even these kinds of high-earner millionaires have failed to reach financial escape velocity.

With few exceptions, only people who have thoughtfully invested their earnings into income-producing assets over long periods can reach financial escape velocity. A person who has achieved financial escape velocity is someone who has accomplished three things. First, on the asset side, they have healthy cash reserves—a diversified portfolio of income-producing assets that give them almost infinite ability to weather economic storms and unexpected setbacks. Second, their assets produce a river of cash flow that fuels a very comfortable standard of living and enables continued investment and net worth growth. Third, and most importantly, the energy required to maintain all of this, due to their financial altitude and speed, is dramatically less than what was required at the initial liftoff.

Using complicated math, scientists can pinpoint a distance from Earth and the speed required to reach escape velocity in a rocket. Since every person's situation is different, we cannot pinpoint the dollar amount or investment return rate needed for you to reach financial escape velocity. However, my hope in defining financial escape velocity is that you can shoot for an economic altitude and financial velocity where you can throttle back on your time and energy invested in growing your wealth, enjoy the fruit of your labor, and watch your wealth rocket continue to soar toward the heavens. More about that later in the final HACKER method step R: "Review, Rework, Repeat, and Reward."

THE FIVE BOOSTERS OF THE REAL ESTATE INVESTING ROCKET

Just as many different kinds of rockets have successfully launched from Earth into space and accomplished escape velocity, there are many different investment vehicles one can ride to financial escape velocity. However, as stated earlier, I believe that real estate is the best escape velocity vehicle with the most stable track record of stunning success. A multimillionaire friend of mine likes to say, "You can make more money by building a successful business than investing in real estate. The problem is, only 10% of businesses succeed whereas 90% of real estate succeeds." In the remainder of this chapter, I am going to outline my argument for why real estate is one of the best ways to build wealth. To do that, let's return to the rocket analogy.

Picture one of the early rockets sitting upright on the launching pad. These rockets had a nose cone and a slender tapered body surrounded by three fins at the bottom that held the rocket upright. These early rockets contained all the fuel in the main tube and created thrust out of its single engine at the bottom. When launched, they would fly high and fast, but they would reach a point where the fuel ran out and gravity overpowered the momentum, and it crashed back to earth.

Once humans decided we wanted to escape Earth's gravity, we needed rockets with a lot more power and speed. We started adding booster rockets around the central rocket. Picture Nasa's Space Shuttle or SpaceX's Falcon Heavy. In this analogy, the central rocket is our net worth. Since we are not happy with merely launching only to crash back to earth, we need to strap some powerful boosters to the side of our central rocket. There are five primary forces at work in the creation of wealth through real estate, so picture five boosters strapped to the outside of your net worth rocket. Each booster carries a propellant and an engine that add thrust to our trajectory to reach financial escape velocity. Let's take a close look at each booster.

Booster #1 - Cash Flow

The first and most obvious booster strapped to our net worth rocket is cash flow. Everyone's investing strategy is different, and therefore, the importance of the cash flow booster varies. People who make smaller incomes may put more emphasis on buying assets that produce a higher cash flow to supplement their lifestyle immediately. People who have more time and aren't in need of a lot of cash in the short term may be willing to invest in assets that will go up in value faster but may not produce a lot of cash flow upfront. The fact remains, however, that no net worth rocket can escape financial gravity without producing some cash flow.

In real estate, cash flows come from rents collected minus the outflows required to keep the property in a condition that it can generate rental income. The typical cash flow statement of a simple single-family home might look like this:

INFLOWS

Rental Income	$2,000.00
Application Fee Income	$75.00
Total Inflows	**$2075.00**

OUTFLOWS

Property Management	$200.00
Mortgage Interest	$888.00
Mortgage Principal	$92.00
Property Taxes	$103.00
Homeowners Insurance	$35.00
Repairs & Maintenance	$298.00
Misc.	$82.00
Total Outflows	**$1,698.00**

NET CASH FLOWS $377.00

In this scenario, the property owner will receive $377.00 from his real estate investment this month. As with almost any investment, not every month will look the same. There may even be months where the outflows far exceed the inflows. However, a properly analyzed and managed real estate investment will produce more inflows than outflows over the long term.

In most cases, one single-family home turned into a rental property won't change an investor's life. In the scenario above, the investor gets to keep just under $400 per month. But an investor that has ten properties like that will be pocketing $3,770 each month. Someone with 100 of those will bank $37,700 each month, and so on. It's relatively easy to look at your ultimate financial escape velocity number and work backwards to the number of rental properties you'll need to reach that financial altitude and velocity.

Booster #2 - Appreciation

First, let's explore the terms appreciation, depreciation, and inflation and discuss how they are related and different. Appreciation is a term that means the rate at which a thing increases in value. Depreciation is a term that means the rate at which a physical thing ages and deteriorates, and therefore loses value. Inflation is a term that means the rate at which a currency inflates or loses purchasing power. All three terms apply to real estate, and all three are forces that are working at some level all the time.

In an economy with high inflation, real estate values will usually increase faster than in times with lower inflation. While most investors will agree that inflation is not something we wish for, as it has broader negative effects on the overall economy, owners of real estate tend to fare very well during periods of high inflation. This is simply because as a currency loses purchasing power, the cost to replace old houses with new ones will go up. Inflation causes lumber, concrete, and labor costs to rise, and therefore, building new real estate costs more. When new real estate costs rise, owners of existing real estate can get more money for their older property.

Inflation is one form of appreciation, but not the only reason real estate may increase in value. Real estate in a location that becomes more popular may go up in value faster than the rate of inflation. Astute investors are always trying to purchase real estate in areas they think will increase in value fastest. Many investors try to figure out where the "path of progress" is in a given market and buy real estate there. Others look at historical appreciation rates and buy in the zip codes or neighborhoods that tend to appreciate better than others. Investors who place a higher value on appreciation over cash flow may look at multi-state geographical regions with higher-than-average appreciation rates and invest there. It is also possible for real estate to have negative appreciation. This means that a property could go down in value based on lost desirability or bad economic conditions. Don't confuse negative appreciation, a drop in value of the land and building, with depreciation or deterioration of a building. They are not the same thing.

It's also important to understand the concept of highest and best use and how that ties into appreciation rates. Buying the most valuable piece of land in Manhattan to build a 1,200-square-foot, three-bedroom house would not be the highest and best use of that land. In fact, that kind of foolish decision would actually make the land worth less because an investor would have to pay to bulldoze the house so that he could rebuild a skyscraper there instead.

Conversely, buying the cheapest land you can find in rural upstate New York would be the worst place to build a skyscraper. Nobody would rent from you, and you would lose all the money you put into the project. While these two scenarios are unrealistic extremes, the concept is very important to grasp. Astute investors try to invest in real estate that marries a great location with the absolute best building for that location. This will ensure the best appreciation rates long term.

Well-maintained real estate located in prime areas or in the path of progress is key to your quest to reach financial escape velocity. As with the cash flow booster, each investor must assess their priorities when determining which booster deserves more weight. The chart below shows a generalized correlation between cash flow versus appreciation rates. In most cases, markets or areas with high cash flow do not also have high appreciation rates and vice versa. Many investors say they demand both high cash flow and high appreciation, but the truth is, while possible, such a scenario is not normal or easy to accomplish.

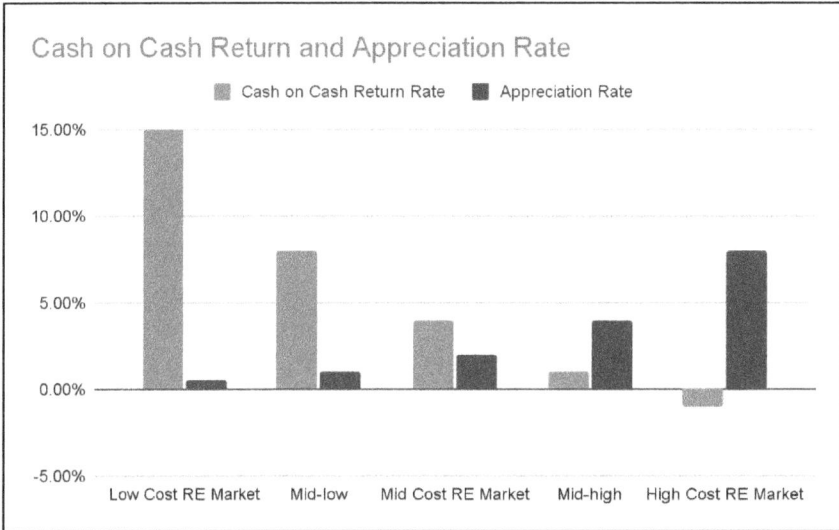

All things being equal, high appreciation rates tend to benefit investors more than high cash flows over the long haul, in part due to the leverage of real estate-backed debt, which we'll discuss next.

Booster #3 - Leverage

The third booster on our net worth rocket, to put it bluntly, is debt. It's not just any debt, however. It's debt taken out that is backed by the real estate owned. I like to use the term "leverage" to describe this kind of debt because the root word of leverage is lever. Levers are tools that help us accomplish hard tasks, and debt just has a negative stigma attached to it. As with any debt, great care should be taken when acquiring it. That said, debt in the form of leverage, perhaps more than the other boosters, will enable you to reach financial escape velocity. There are four primary reasons why this is the case.

The first reason debt is a vital wealth booster is that it reduces the amount of money you need in order to start or continue investing. For example, if you purchase a house for $200,000 but get an 80% loan on that house, you only have to come up with $40,000 instead of the full $200,000. If you follow Dave Ramsey's formula for investing, you'd have to save up 100% of the purchase price of a rental home before buying it. That would take most people many years to accomplish. Imagine if you decided to invest in large multi-family apartment complexes. You're not likely to stockpile the $20 million needed to purchase a 100-unit complex in your entire lifetime.

It is true that purchasing real estate with only cash and no debt is safer than using debt. However, acquiring debt at reasonable loan-to-value (or LTV) ratios coupled with the long-term stability of real estate values in most investable markets makes acquiring debt an acceptable risk for serious investors.

The amount of debt you should put on any investment is a formula you personally need to come up with. Such a formula needs to balance your desire for wealth growth in the long term and staying financially secure in the near term. The chart below is a simple way to visualize real-estate backed debt-to-value ratios and how they correlate to risk.

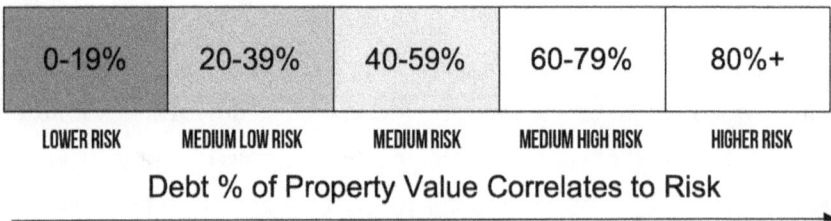

0-19%	20-39%	40-59%	60-79%	80%+
LOWER RISK	MEDIUM LOW RISK	MEDIUM RISK	MEDIUM HIGH RISK	HIGHER RISK

Debt % of Property Value Correlates to Risk

Most banks have loan packages between 60 and 90% of LTV. Some loans subsidized by the U.S. government can qualify for even 97% or more of the property's value. Remember that the higher your loan amount, the higher your loan payments. Also, realize that real estate can decrease in value during down economic cycles. If your loan is 97% LTV today, but in the next year the economy struggles and your house loses 5% of its value, you would owe the bank more money than your house is worth.

All this talk about risk and debt may be overwhelming to someone without experience in real estate. However, I want you to take a pause here and read and internalize the following statement:

The actual market value of real estate only matters on three specific days. Those days are:

1) The day you buy it

2) The day it appraises when you refinance

3) The day you sell it.

Obviously, you need to purchase the property at a great price. So, price matters the day you buy it.

If you ever get the property refinanced after the initial purchase, the value of the property matters at the time that the bank gets it appraised. The appraisal valuation will determine how much money you can pull out of the property.

It goes without saying that the price clearly matters on the day you sell it as well. All the rest of the days that you own a piece of real estate, however, the value of your real estate is almost irrelevant. Outside those three days, the number that is most important is your cash flow. All things being equal, if your property is cash flow positive, the value of the property and the loan balance attached to it just simply don't matter.

I know very successful people who panicked and sold property in the 2008 housing crash and lost a ton of money even though their rents were covering their expenses. Panicky investors who overreact in the short term usually lose. Long-term strategic investors with strong cash flows almost always win.

The second reason debt is vital to wealth building relates to how debt can increase your return on investment. Let's use the hypothetical rental scenario we created earlier in the chapter to explain this phenomenon. Say you buy a rental property for $200,000 with all cash and no loan. Let's also say your tenants pay $2,000 per month in rent, and your costs to manage the property are $800. You have a positive cash flow of $1,200 per month. If you decided to finance that property with a 30-year bank loan at 80% LTV at 5.5% interest, you'd add $733 per month in interest and $175 per month in principal. Your cash flow with the loan would drop to $292 per month. On the surface, nobody wants to bring in less cash flow. But to understand why debt in this case is so powerful, you need to start calculating your return on investment.

Without a loan, you will have had to use $200,000 of your money in order to get $1,200 per month in cash flow. The annualized return on investment (ROI) in this scenario is:

$$(\$1200 * 12) / \$200,000 = 7.2\%$$

However, with an 80% LTV loan, you only had to invest $40,000 of your own money and are getting $292 per month in cash flow. The annualized ROI in this scenario is:

$$($292*12) / $40,000 = 8.8\%$$

If you have $200,000 to invest and you decide to go safe and pay cash for a $200,000 house, you would buy that house and be out of money. However, if you decide to leverage your capital, you could buy five houses each with just $40,000 down. Now you have five houses, all earning a higher return rate and higher cash flows on your investment. Instead of earning $1,200 on just one house, you're bringing in $1,460 with five rental homes.

Additionally, owning five homes spreads your risk across five properties versus just one. If your one and only house has a major repair need and cannot be rented for a period of time, you might be in trouble. However, if just one of five rental homes goes offline for a repair, it's much less painful to work through.

The third reason why debt is a powerful booster for your net worth rocket is the simple fact that your tenants pay off your mortgage for you. Remember that in all of our cash flow estimates, we include both interest and principal payments in our calculation. Successful real estate purchases spin off enough rent to put positive cash flow in your pocket every month AND pay off your debt at the same time. I remember the month when the combined principal payments my tenants were paying each month (thus reducing my mortgage balance) were higher than my monthly salary. The thrill of that day helped cement in my mind the power of debt on cash-flowing real estate.

The fourth reason why leverage on good real estate is a positive thing has to do with what I call the inflation multiplication effect. As we have illustrated earlier, if you buy a $200,000 house with all cash, you have

$200,000 invested. If you get an 80% loan, you only have $40,000 invested. Assuming the home rises with the sixty-year average rate of inflation of 3.8%, your home will go up in value by $7,600 in its first year. A $7,600 increase on a $200,000 invested is a 3.8% return. However, a $7,600 gain on a $40,000 investment is a 19% return! As the chart below visually illustrates, while your property goes up in value, the return on your initial investment continues to increase.

Appreciation Effect With Leverage

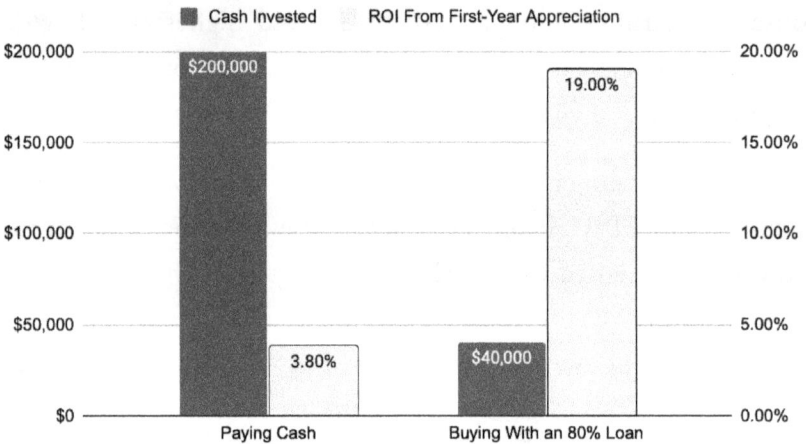

Legend: ■ Cash Invested   ROI From First-Year Appreciation

	Paying Cash	Buying With an 80% Loan
Cash Invested	$200,000	$40,000
ROI From First-Year Appreciation	3.80%	19.00%

Booster #4 - Legal Tax Shelter

There are entire books written about the subject of how real estate can be used to reduce your annual tax bill. There are creative ways out there to use real estate to even reduce the taxes you pay for W2 jobs. To keep things simple, I just want to briefly touch on how current U.S. tax laws can shield your cash flow profits from most, if not all, federal and state income taxes. I say "current," as laws change all the time, and there's no guarantee these tax allowances will remain on the books. To know for sure, consult with a real estate CPA or investigate the tax code yourself.

Returning to our cash flow statement, let's assume you have a property that is generating $370 in positive cash flow every month, which is the amount of money going into your pocket. When you prepare your tax return, the government is not interested in the amount of money that goes into your pocket. Rather, they want to know what your actual income and expense was. Their formula does not allow you to count the payments you made to principal on any loans. That's because even though that money left your pocket, it still benefits you in a reduced loan amount. However, they do let you count depreciation expense, which didn't affect the money that went into your pocket. Remember that depreciation is just the acknowledgment that your building has deteriorated with time and use. The government allows you to depreciate the full value of most buildings to $0.00 over the span of 27 ½ years.

Let's return to our hypothetical property worth $200,000. You determine that the land alone is worth $50,000. This means you are valuing the building at $150,000. In this scenario, the IRS allows you to show a non-cash depreciation expense on your tax return of $5,455 every year for 27 ½ years ($5,455 x 27.5 = $150,000). Using the same hypothetical monthly cash flow statement from earlier in the chapter, let's look at an annualized tax income and expense statement we would use to create our tax return.

Annual Tax Income & Expense Statement

Rental Income	$24,000.00
Non-Refundable Deposit	$900.00
Total Income	**$24,900.00**

Taxable Expenses

Property Management	$2,400.00
Mortgage Interest	$10,656.00

Property Taxes	$1236.00
Homeowners Insurance	$420.00
Repairs & Maintenance	$3,576.00
Misc.	$3,108.00
Depreciation Expense	$5,455.00
Total Outflows	**$26,851.00**
Net Taxable Income/(Loss)	**($1,951.00)**

In summary, this property puts $292 in cash in our pockets every month, which is $3,504 over the course of a year. But the IRS allows us to show them a loss of $1,951.00. When we show a loss, we don't have to pay taxes and are even able to apply that loss to passive income in future years.

It's important to understand why the U.S. government allows this kind of tax sheltering. Politicians decided a long time ago that they didn't want the government to be in the business of building housing. Failed attempts at building "projects" in some inner cities caused lawmakers to create tax incentives to get investors like you and me to do that work for them.

So, the next time someone accuses investors of using "loopholes" to get rich, kindly help them understand that they aren't loopholes at all. They are incentives created intentionally by politicians to get us to provide Americans with homes.

Before we advance to the fifth and final real estate booster, let me conclude this section by pointing out that debt is part of the calculation on sheltering your taxes. I am not a political insider and I cannot say for sure, but it seems to me that lawmakers came up with the 27 ½ years for depreciation to more or less match the most common home loans of 25 to 30 years. If you think critically, the lifespan of most houses is well over 27 ½ years. Many of the homes I own are older than that, and they all have original foundations, studs, etc. So, my theory is that the government wanted to help investors buy property on debt and use depreciation expense to "cover" their debt and operating expenses. The bottom line is, if you decided not to leverage your properties with debt, and therefore not be able to write off interest expense, your ability to shelter your income from taxes would diminish

Booster #5 - Honey I Shrunk the Debt!

In 1989, a movie came out called *Honey, I Shrunk The Kids*. The plot of this silly movie was that a geeky scientist invented a laser-shooting machine that could shrink solid objects to a fraction of their original size. One day, the shrinker gun accidentally pointed at and shot their three children and shrunk them down to the size of bugs. The rest of the movie is the attempt of the mom and dad to save them from getting hunted by the family cat and to restore them to normal size. To help you understand this fifth and final booster on our net worth rocket, I want you to imagine that real estate investors have invented a contraption that can shrink the relative size of our debt. Our debt-shrinking machine is built with fixed-rate amortized loans, macro-economic inflation, and most importantly, time. When we mix all of these ingredients together, our debt shrinks before our eyes.

When I say our debt shrinks, I am not referring to the actual balance discussed in booster #4. I am referring to the impact of the debt payments relative to our economic situation over time. If you're lost, stick with me here.

Let's paint a scenario once again using our $200,000 rental house. Pretend that while the house is worth $200,000 today, we bought it twenty years ago for $110,000. Let's say that when we purchased the house, we took out a 30-year fixed-rate loan at 5% APR at an LTV of 80%. In this scenario, our principal and interest payments would be $476.70 per month. Twenty years ago, the rent collected on that house barely covered that $476.70 mortgage and the operating expenses. With twenty years of rent inflation, however, that $476.70 is a pittance compared to the $2,000 per month in rent we get now. Once more, let's take a look at our cash flow statement, but let's replace the mortgage interest and principal costs of a new mortgage with this twenty-year-old mortgage to see the power of how time and inflation reduce the absolute impact of debt on real estate:

Inflows

Rental Income	$2,000.00
Application Fee Income	$75.00
Total Inflows	**$2075.00**

Outflows

Property Management	$200.00
Mortgage Interest	$195.00
Mortgage Principal	$282.00
Property Taxes	$103.00
Homeowners Insurance	$35.00
Repairs & Maintenance	$298.00
Misc.	$82.00
Total Outflows	**$1,195.00**
Net Cash Flows	**$880.00**

Not only does our mortgage payment become a smaller and smaller percentage of the rents you collect, but the balance of the loan keeps getting paid down while the value of the property is likely going up. If you had simply made the minimum payment on your original loan for twenty years, your balance would have reduced by $43,856 while your equity grew by $90,000. That's a $133,856 increase in your net worth, not counting the positive cash flow over the last twenty years. In this scenario, you're holding a building worth $200,000 with less than $45,000 in debt and very strong cash flow. Considering you only paid $22,200 down for that property, you are sitting in a very strong cash-flowing position with extremely low debt risk.

The bottom line on this booster is that the nonstop drumbeat of time coupled with inflation and land appreciation constantly shrink the impact that fixed-rate debt has on your investments. In conclusion, I have analyzed hundreds of different kinds of investments in my lifetime. Many of them have one or more of the "boosters" that real estate has, but, to my knowledge, none of them have all five. This is what, in my humble opinion, makes real estate a superior vehicle to reach financial escape velocity.

CHAPTER 15

THE THREE SIMPLE STEPS TO START INVESTING

YOU CAN'T LEARN TO RIDE A BIKE FROM A WEBINAR.

A friend of mine named Josh Kinney came to me and asked for $50,000. He wanted to partner with me to buy some bare land just behind a new Walmart. The seller of the land had just completed construction of 100 apartment units, and this little slice of land was too small to fit another block of twenty apartments, so it wasn't worth his effort to build it out. Josh said he wanted to buy the land, draw up plans for two four-plexes, get the plan approved through the city, and sell it to a builder. He already had an agreed-on price with a builder at double our cost. He anticipated it would take nine months from purchasing to the completion of construction.

At first, I was skeptical. It felt risky to depend on the builder and then wait for a buyer to come along so we could get our money back. I also wondered why it was so easy to double my money in such a short amount of time without really doing very much work. I found it strange that so much value could be created just by filing some paperwork and paying an architect to draw up some pretty standard four-plex plans. Instead of giving into the fear of what I didn't understand, I invited Josh to our favorite IHOP to explain the process to me over breakfast.

In an attempt to calm my fears, Josh told me that deals like this happen ALL THE TIME. As I have become a better investor, I've been able to be involved in more deals like this. Josh explained that the land was too small for some things, too large for others, and wasn't correctly zoned for something in between. It also needed someone with certain skills and city connections to convert it into something valuable. After Josh explained all the nuances of this parcel, my admiration for Josh grew. He had been investing his money in real estate for long enough that he was able to instantly see opportunities that other people saw as problems not worth pursuing.

So, Josh, another investor, and I put our money in, bought the land, and put the plan into action. A little more than nine months later, my $50,000 investment turned into $94,350. Not only did our partnership almost double our money, Josh's builder friend made over $200,000 on the sale of his two newly built four-plexes! Let it sink in for a minute that a piece of land worth $150,000 before our project created nearly $350,000 of profit in less than a year.

What's equally intriguing to me is that everyone involved in this project had reason to celebrate a victory! The original seller of the land was thrilled to offload "useless" land for $150,000. Our partnership was very happy to double our money in nine months. Josh's builder friend was ecstatic to pocket $200,000 for his labor. The investor who bought the four-plexes was happy to put his money to work in brand-new buildings. The tenants who signed leases were pleased to live in brand-new, higher-end apartments in a great part of town. Even the city was happy with the project because it added affordable housing during a housing shortage.

Another lesson I want to highlight here is to show investing as not just a method to get rich, but also as a valuable service to the community. The idea that business people only make money at the expense of the poor masses is an incorrect and oversimplified view of capitalism. The purest form of capitalism brings people of varying skills and experience into voluntary transactions to turn something of little value into something of greater value. It's magical! What I want is for you to learn how to identify opportunities that abound, not only to build wealth but to become one of those value-adding members of the community.

In order for you to begin to see and seize opportunities around you, you need to do three things. First, you need to be looking. **Opportunities don't actually fall in your lap, as the saying goes. Rather, opportunities pass through your line of sight. If you aren't trained to see them, opportunities will approach you, stare you in the face, and if you don't grab them, fly right on by.** Second, you need to be able to assess the opportunity and decipher the potential return on your investment if you act on the opportunity. Not every deal you see is one you should take. Finally, once you're satisfied that the potential return is greater than the risks, you need to take action. Let's explore these three steps to taking advantage of an opportunity one by one.

STEP ONE: RECOGNIZING WHEN OPPORTUNITY ARISES

One time I went to a sales training seminar. Ironically, the title of the seminar was "You Can't Learn to Ride a Bike at a Seminar." What they were trying to say was that the only way to learn to ride a bike, or how to be successful as a salesperson, is to get out in the real world and learn through trial and error. Riding a bike, learning how to sell products or services, and recognizing investing opportunities can only come from repeated attempts, many of which end in scraped knees and bruised egos, at least in the beginning.

Speaking of scraped knees, I want to tell you a story. Soon after Josh and I doubled our money on that little slice of land, a man named Danilo from one of the churches we had started in Ecuador came up to me and invited the pastor and me to come see his rose plantation. It turns out that Ecuador is the largest exporter of roses in the world. This church of ours happened to be in the middle of the most perfect soil and climate for year-round rose production on earth. As soon as we arrived at the plantation, Danilo gave us the VIP tour. We saw people clipping roses and packaging them for shipment. We saw the storage warehouses and several refrigerated transport trucks lined up at the docking bays. At the end of our tour, we saw men loading crates of roses into a sea container bound for Russia. It was an impressive operation.

Then Danilo invited us into his office and confessed that he needed our help. He explained that he landed some huge unexpected orders and didn't have the funds to fulfill them. If he passed up the order, he'd lose over $100,000 profit. He needed a $50,000 loan and promised to repay it and an additional $25,000 fee in just sixty days. One of my favorite sayings to my kids is, "I was born at night, but not last night!" Immediately, my intuition said, "No way"! I didn't like mixing my non-profit work with business, and I had just barely met this guy. Most of all, there was just too much risk, mostly because it felt too good to be true.

Before I could say no, however, Danilo slapped a couple of documents in front of me. They were titles to two vehicles. One was for a double-decker tourism bus and the other for a semi-truck with a refrigerator trailer. Danilo said, "As collateral, I'll sign over title to these two vehicles, worth over $100,000. I'll deliver them to the church, and if I don't pay you the full $75,000 in sixty days, these vehicles are yours. You can sell them, hire them out, whatever you want." The pastor and I said we'd get back to him within a day or two.

On our drive back, we discussed the opportunity. After a lot of back and forth, we decided to do some checking on the vehicles. If everything checked out, I'd find investors, and we'd do the deal. I promised to donate 10% of the gain to the church. The pastor's job was to take the vehicles to a mechanic he trusted to have them thoroughly checked out for any surprise problems. If that checked out, he was to do a title search to make sure the vehicles didn't have any liens or other issues that would cause us to not be able to sell them if Danilo didn't come through. Finally, we looked at the local online vehicle sales website, and the valuations Danilo gave us checked out.

I called my buddy Josh and pitched the deal to him. I offered to put up $25,000, and if he'd do $25,000, we'd split the profits 50/50. I was eager to return the favor to Josh and help him make some money even quicker than our four-plex lot deal. Josh agreed, the vehicles got the green light from the mechanic and the title search, and we wired $50,000 to the Bella Rosa Company in Ibarra, Ecuador.

To put it mildly, things didn't go as planned. Long story short, Danilo never paid us back, and if I had to guess, I'd say he never intended on doing so. In essence, he sold us two vehicles. Fair enough, I thought. The vehicles were worth more than the loan balance and interest, so I figured we might just come out really well here with a little bit of effort and a little more time than planned. That was wishful thinking.

We found a buyer for the bus right off the bat and negotiated a price of $40,000. We were pretty excited, expecting to make even more than the $25,000 in the original deal. The buyer came to the church, checked it out, and made a phone call. He got off the phone and said, "I'm sorry, but this bus isn't registered with the tourism office. It doesn't have the permit required to be hired out professionally. It can only be used privately. Without that permit, it's only worth $20,000 to maybe $25,000." Four months later and not just a few majorly stressful discussions with city officials, other buyers, and tourism companies, we finally admitted that this guy was right. Danilo dumped a problem bus on our laps. We ended up selling it for $18,000. That was skinned knee number one.

Not too long after the bus buyer pulled the wool off our eyes, the pastor called me and said, "We have more bad news…I found a major problem with the semi-truck." He went on to explain that it was true that the title was free of liens, but there was a tax embargo on it that wasn't reported to the agency we used for the title search. Neither the pastor nor I had any idea that we had to look in two places to verify that the vehicle was unencumbered. I asked the pastor how much the embargo was for. He didn't want to answer me. After some coaxing, he muttered, "Just under $18,000." Holy rose farm, Batman! We are going to lose the entire tour bus sale just to pay the taxes on the semi! And that's exactly what we did. We took all the money from the bus sale, paid the taxes, and set out to sell the semi-truck.

At this point, all hope for profit was lost. Now, we were just hoping to get our $50,000 capital back. After the thirty days it took to get the title clean, we listed the truck for $55,000, ready to accept $50,000 just to be done with the ordeal. It sat for thirty days without so much as one phone call. We lowered the price to $52,500. It sat for two more weeks with a couple of calls, but no buyers. We drove the truck down to the largest vehicle liquidation sale in Ecuador with the price of $49,000 on the window. The pastor and I sat out in the hot sun all day hassling, passersby like street corner beggars, trying to find a buyer. The drive home in the unsold truck was mostly silent.

We dropped the price to $42,500 and after about four months, we sold the truck for $40,000 to its lucky new owner. I called Josh and apologized for my error and pledged to pay the losses. I gave Josh his money back, and I took the $10,000 hit myself.

I share this story with you for two reasons. First, it's important to know that you will not bat .1000. The good news is, your losses tend to happen less frequently the longer you're in the game. The second reason I shared this story with you is because the losses like these are the ones that have made me a much better investor, and the same will happen for you. The memory of the pain of the losses is ten times stronger than the thrill of a win. Nobody likes to tell their stories of losses because nobody wants to look stupid, and nobody wants to relive the anguish associated with the loss. I'm convinced that the massacre at the rose plantation and other similar loser deals I have done have both saved me and made me millions.

You can only learn to see opportunities once you've notched some victories AND some losses. You can work alongside peers or listen to mentors. But there's no replacement for falling off your bike, skinning your knee, and getting right back up on the seat to try again.

The other good news is that once you've taken a few swings at opportunities, your vision will get sharper as new deals come along. As you hone your specific skill set, you'll see things that others won't, and if you act fast, you can start to see incredible returns on your investment and watch your wealth snowball.

STEP TWO: DETERMINE YOUR RETURN ON INVESTMENT

In real estate, we say that the profit is made in the purchase. What that means is the key to doing well in real estate is picking the right property to buy in the first place. This reinforces the overused but partially valuable cliche of the three rules of real estate being 1) location, 2) location, and 3) location. But location alone really is not enough. You must also do what is called underwriting. Underwriting is a fancy real estate word for due diligence, which is also a fancy phrase meaning, "will the project make money."

If the only rule in real estate was location, everyone on earth would just get into a giant bidding war for that iconic wedge-shaped building in Times Square, often cited as the most valuable retail property in the United States. But even the most valuable retail space in the country can only produce so much income. The income that prime location generates will determine its value. So, if we were to pay more than the value supported by the rent tenants are willing to pay for that prime location, we would go bankrupt. In effect, the only three rules of real estate should actually be 1) underwriting, 2) underwriting, and 3) underwriting. I'm not saying we ignore location. What I am saying is that a strong underwriting will factor in the location and a hundred other factors in their analysis of that property. In fact, the first field in my personal underwriting spreadsheet is location score. I will only go through the effort of underwriting properties with a location score within a certain range.

Due to the high complexity of real estate investing, not to mention all the other asset classes in which someone can invest, I cannot give you the underwriting step by step here. I do offer a series of underwriting calculators at www.TheUnexpectedInvestor.com/calculators.

That said, the formula for return on investment (ROI) is simple:

- Total Profit from An Investment (X) minus Original Capital Invested (Y) = Investment Gain (Z)
- Investment Gain (Z) divided by Original Capital Invested (Y) = Return On Investment (ROI)

Expressed as a two step formula:

X-Y=Z
Z/Y = ROI

Let's use Josh's four-plex land development deal in this example. The original capital invested just from me was $50,000. The total received from the investment was $94,350. So:

$94,350 (X) - $50,000 (Y) = $44,350 (Z).
$44,350 (Z)/$50,000 (Y) = 88.7% (ROI)

My personal ROI on the four-plex land was 88.7%. However, how do we know that is a good ROI? If it took us ten years to get that return, it wouldn't be nearly as impressive as getting that return in just nine months. To make the ROI formula even more informative, we need to convert it to an annualized return on investment. Since we realized an 88.7% gain in nine months, I can simply divide 88.7% by nine, then multiply that number by twelve. That comes out to 118% annualized ROI. In other words, if I can consistently get an 88.7% ROI every nine months, I could expect to earn 118% every year. I'm not saying that replicating that return can be repeated forever. I'm simply using the annualized ROI number to help me more adequately compare one opportunity to another.

For a little dose of humility, the ROI formula also works for losses, so let's run the ROI formula for the massacre at the rose plantation.

$$\$40,000 \ (X) - \$50,000 \ (Y) = -\$10,000 \ (Z)$$
$$-\$10,000 \ (Z)/\$50,000 \ (Y) = -20\% \ (ROI)$$

My return on investment was a negative 20%. Since it took us about a year to get out of that mess, our ROI is actually nearly the same as our annualized ROI.

STEP THREE: TAKE ACTION

For every person who takes the leap into the world of investing, there are dozens or even hundreds of people who talk about it but never do. I can't possibly know all the reasons that keep people from building wealth and finding financial freedom. All I can do is hypothesize.

One of my theories on what keeps people from taking action revolves around our relationship with money. From the day we are born until the day we perish from this earth, we hear things about money. For too many, money is always presented as this highly scarce commodity. There's never enough money available to pay the bills and then enjoy life on top. So, our default is to hoard money as if our lives depended on it. We get so obsessed with keeping a tight grip on money that we develop an unhealthy relationship with money. It's almost as if money is locked up in this holy shrine called a bank account, and taking some out for anything but the bare necessities is committing the worst possible sin. The sin, however, is our inability to release our death grip on money and let it start working for us.

Another theory is that some people lack the self-confidence to make wise investments. All I can say to you here is that every investor, indeed, every human being, struggles with feelings of inadequacy in some ways. This is one of the most normal human realities. Put yourself around people who believe in you and who know what they're talking about in the asset class in which you are interested. Allow them to coach you and encourage you until your confidence grows to the point that you're willing to take the leap.

There is good news for both the people who have an unhealthy grip on their money and the people who lack self-confidence. Once you actually start investing and learn the lessons that only come from trial and error, your grip will loosen, and your confidence will soar. It won't take very long before you become an expert in your asset class and you are mentoring the next apprehensive aspiring investor to take the leap!

As you gain momentum in investing, you'll start to experience something almost magical. A few years ago, I was showing my wife how our net worth was starting to grow at an increasingly quick rate. She said, "Wow, it's snowballing." In other words, our investment strategies had started to multiply exponentially. Our frugal living, dedication to investing, long-term strategy, and skill in picking good investments all started to pay big dividends. The key to hacking into the wealthy class is not obtaining a 10% annual return in the stock market. It's predicated on the idea that, with enough time and experience, you can create an exponential acceleration of the value of your assets, which is what we will explore in the next HACKER section, "Exponentiality."

EXPONENTIALITY

CHAPTER 16

INFINITY, I WIN!

TRADING TIME FOR MONEY IS FOOL'S FOLLY.

DOCTORS AREN'T THE TOP OF THE FOOD CHAIN

Growing up, I always had the understanding that the people who sat atop the economic ladder were doctors and lawyers. A rung below them were the really smart people like engineers, accountants, and computer programmers. Another couple steps down were nurses, physical therapists, and dental hygienists. I assumed that the higher I was willing to climb that ladder, the more money I could make and the wealthier I could become. I think it's safe to say that my perception of the professional structure in America is not unique. Most people can at least understand how I came to these conclusions, if not have the same perspective.

In my late teens, as I was contemplating the direction of my life, I remember an internal discussion I had in my head where I contemplated the likelihood of reaching that top rung. I wasn't interested in being a lawyer, but what about being a doctor? I liked the idea of wearing a white coat with a stethoscope around my neck. The cherry on top was that doctors have the noble mission of healing people from what ails them. While I saw doctors as having the maximum earning potential, I doubted I was smart enough to make it through the education and training process to become a doctor. To make myself feel better about my perceived inferior intellect, I decided not to pursue medicine simply due to the "extra years of college required." It was easier on my ego to scoff at the time med school students were wasting in the classroom than to admit I probably didn't qualify.

Looking back, I ask myself why the ladder of success seems to only have these college degree jobs at the top? Why are all of these careers ones that require 60-80 hours of work per week? Why isn't real estate investor, inventor, or serial entrepreneur on the list? Who is responsible for creating this image of the ladder to success in our minds, and why? Regardless of the answers to those questions, I'm here to take that ladder down and chop it up into firewood.

The concept is simple. Every single career on that ladder to success requires the person in that career to trade their time for money. Any time you are trading time for money, you are capped at your growth potential. I understand that doctors make a lot of money per hour, especially compared to bookkeepers or administrative assistants. Nonetheless, the easiest path for doctors to earn more is to take more patients and work longer hours. As an investor, however, if you can learn the art of investing for infinite returns, your growth has no limit, and the time you have to invest for each increment of growth diminishes to near zero over time.

For all the doctors reading this, I can see you shaking your fist at me right now. Perhaps you take issue with my argument that the only way for a doctor to earn more is to work more. Maybe you have figured out how to bring up-and-coming doctors into your practice, pushing the workload off to them while increasing your take-home profits. If that's you, lower your fist and accept my congratulations on retiring (or at least semi-retiring) from being a doctor and becoming an entrepreneur. You have learned how to escape the trap of trading time for money. Anyone who has the skills to cast a vision that attracts other professionals to do the leg work and pass some of the profits up to themselves has cracked the code that I have been working on my entire adult life. You need to stop thinking of earning money being correlated directly to your labor and start figuring out how to create perpetual wealth-building machines.

INFINITY, I WIN!

First, I want to share a real-world scenario of creating infinite returns. The very first property I bought was a duplex in Nampa, Idaho. I bought it in 1996 with $2,500 of my money. Since this was back in the days of extremely loose lending practices, the bank lent me the rest. When I finally sold the duplex in 2014, I looked at the profit and loss statement for the eighteen years I held that property, and I barely broke even. I thought back to the countless clogged toilets, tripped breakers, broken door knobs, and tenant screenings, and I started to get flustered. All that effort and no cash flow to show for it! However, the cash flow was only one factor. I had sold the property for $46,000 more than I paid for it, and my loan balance had been significantly reduced. At closing, I had a check for over $100,000! So my initial $2,500 invested turned into $100,000! That's roughly a 4,000% return! Even spreading that return over the eighteen years I owned the duplex, I was looking at a 222% return per year!

While a 222% annual return is impressive, it's still not infinite. I still had $2,500 of my money invested. To achieve infinite returns, you must ultimately pull your original investment out while still holding onto the asset that is generating profits and/or equity growth. Had I taken my $97,500 profit and spent it, the story would have ended with healthy returns, but not infinite returns. Fortunately for me, I didn't spend a dime of that closing check. I took all the money and bought a four-plex through a 1031 exchange.

POP-UP DEFINITION

A 1031 exchange - named after IRS code 1031 that allows real estate to be traded for another property of equal or greater value. The advantage of 1031 exchange is that capital gains taxes on the profits of the sold property can be deferred.

While the duplex didn't produce cash flow for over eighteen years, the four-plex did from the very beginning. After just six months of owning the four-plex, I had recouped my original $2,500 duplex investment. Once I had pocketed the $2,500 in profits, I had now entered into the realm of infinite returns. Here's where the story gets exciting!

Fast forward four years to 2017. The value of the four-plex had shot up another $100,000! I called my mentor and bragged about how much equity I had built up! As any good mentor would do, he told me to quit bragging and stop being dumb. He said, and I quote, "You have way too much equity." I was stunned! How could anyone have too much equity? He convinced me to increase my leverage by refinancing the four-plex to buy more units. I did exactly that. I refinanced and pulled $100,000 out and bought six more units.

Rather than bore you with all the subsequent details, the short version is that my first two units turned into four, then ten and, as of this writing, have grown to twenty-one units worth several million dollars and generating over $100,000 per year in cash flow. I have other projects that have not yet reached infinite returns, but that is always my goal. If you can master the art of infinite returns, your doctor buddies will be begging you to take their money to invest so they can eventually stop trading their time for money. Just like kids on the playground, the first one to claim infinity wins!

BRRRR, IT'S HOT!

In real estate investing, there's a strategy designed around the concept of achieving infinite returns called BRRRR investing. BRRRR is an acronym that stands for Buy, Remodel, Rent, Refinance, Repeat. The most basic premise of the strategy is to find a property that is in bad shape, buy it at a steep discount, remodel it to bring it back to its highest and best potential, rent it out to a tenant, and then refinance it, pulling out all of your purchase and remodel price. Finally, you take the refinance proceeds to go buy the next one and repeat the cycle endlessly. If you are able to get a good enough deal on the purchase and control your remodel costs enough, it is possible to get a cash-out refinance mortgage big enough to cover all of your initial investment. If your rent is large enough to comfortably cover your mortgage, operating expenses, and capital expenditure reserves, then you can witness the power of infinite returns in a much shorter time period than I did with my first duplex.

POP-UP DEFINITION

Capital expenditure reserves - an estimate of future expenses to replace or repair big ticket items. In real estate, these items are roofs, HVAC, Water Heaters, Appliances, etc. All serious investors include capital reserves in their research before buying property and set aside reserves for existing property in their portfolio.

A word of caution on BRRRR investing. Just because you could accomplish an infinite return on a project doesn't mean you necessarily should. It's possible to build up a portfolio of BRRRR'd properties that are too highly leveraged. When (not if) the next economic winter comes, you could find yourself saying, "BRRRR, it's cold outside!" In cold economic times, rents sometimes fall. If your rents fall too low, you could find yourself in a dangerous financial situation because of your BRRRRs.

While infinite returns are one goal we should shoot for, it is not the only goal. Always take other factors into account. For example, what is the lowest debt-to-value ratio you are willing to hold on your portfolio? What is the minimum cash flow you need to justify the time you invest in your portfolio? What is your timeframe for generating enough income to quit your salaried job? Which leads me to my final thoughts on infinite returns: passive investing.

ACTIVE PASSIVE INVESTING

While the term "active passive investing" may sound like an oxymoron, it's a play on words that attempt to make a point. First, let's define passive investing. Passive investing is the act of investing money in projects, funds, or businesses with management and systems in place that you have no say in or responsibility for. Truly passive investments only need your money and, by definition, do not require your time or labor.

You might be tempted to say that owning your own real estate and hiring a property manager would classify as passive investing. Technically and legally, this would be accurate, but if you've ever dealt with a property manager, you painfully know the word "passive" doesn't really describe the situation. Only negligent investors will hire a manager and then check out, and negligent investors will almost surely lose in the end. Smart investors know they have to provide at least some oversight of the team managing their assets.

There are lots of different kinds of passive investing. Buying stocks on Wall Street is passive investing. Parking your money in CDs at the bank is passive. Buying treasury bills from Uncle Sam is passive. More sophisticated passive investments range from multi-family apartment syndications, venture capital investments, and other private equity funds and securities that you can buy from individuals who don't sell their shares on public markets. My advice to you is to start out investing in your own projects to learn the art and science of investing. However, I encourage you to set your sights on a day when you can harvest the profits from your investing career and "actively" seek out the best vehicles to park your money in passive investments. Once you reach this level of investing, you'll begin to truly realize and enjoy the power of infinite and compounding returns on your money.

Since we took the ladder to success down and chopped it into firewood, let's take a fresh look at how we should view the path into the wealthy class from the perspective of infinite returns. The ladder of success is very linear. To become a doctor, there is a very rigid process you have to take, and everyone who wants to be a doctor is crammed into that same process.

Being an investor is the opposite. There are an infinite number of paths you can take to achieve success as an investor. Very few investors have taken the exact same route to success. My advice is to dive into the industry or asset class that most excites you. Find a mentor immediately, then dive into an investment as an owner-operator. I recognize owner-operators technically trade time for money, but think of it as your education. The best way to learn is to do. Once you've found your niche and your investment is profitable, leverage into larger and larger investments. When you feel the time is right, pull your initial investment out and watch the power of infinite returns. When your portfolio is large enough and you find your portfolio kicking off more profits than you need to live, start actively researching ways to passively invest.

CHAPTER 17

INVESTING YOUR BIRTHDAY MONEY

TOMORROW'S PROFIT IS CASHED FROM TODAY'S DECISIONS.

I will never forget the look on my wife's face on one of her first birthdays after we got married. She received as a birthday gift a $50 Visa gift card that could be spent anywhere Visa is accepted. Since the local supermarket accepted Visa, I suggested that she put it toward that week's groceries and save on our food budget. By the look she gave me, you would have thought I had suggested we sell one of our children into slavery. "Hands off MY birthday money!" she growled.

In hindsight, I can't blame her for her reaction. I mistakenly assumed she understood the "unexpected windfall investment" concept. When the same thing happened the next year, I was somehow shocked that she still hadn't learned about unexpected windfall investing! Somewhere around the fourth or fifth such confrontation, I wised up and decided to cast the vision for what unexpected windfall investing is and why it's better than going shopping when cash unexpectedly falls in our laps. It was still met with a chilly frown, but eventually, when our wealth snowball started increasing exponentially and our spending budget with it, the $50 birthday gifts became completely irrelevant to our lifestyle, and the related marital strain disappeared.

When creating your spending budgets, you need to be careful to meet your needs by allocating for vacations, fun family activities, frequent date nights, and even unexpected expenses. In other words, your budget should provide for all of your needs and at least enough wants that you can run the wealth-building marathon without needing additional funds outside the budget. If you stick to the 50/40/10 budget concept, your spending budget will constantly grow year after year. Even when your yearly employment income doesn't go up, you should be able to increase your spending budgets because your investment income boosts your budget growth. So, while $50 in a birthday card is exciting to receive, my advice is to invest 100% of it and all other unexpected windfalls to accelerate your path to building serious wealth.

Windfalls are not just birthday gift cards. They might be insurance overpayment refunds or a $100 bill that Auntie Rose slips in your hand while whispering, "Buy something nice for the kiddos." It might be a bonus at work or a tax refund. Unexpected windfalls happen more often than you might think, and they can and should be used to juice your investment account, not to buy something on impulse that you don't really need. Remember, your 50% spend budget should already have room for birthday gifts and other fun stuff too. Your spending budget should ensure that you can live a secure, happy lifestyle without relying on a lucky break to fill your basic budgetary needs.

One day to unwind, I watched an episode of the TV show Pawn Stars. I get amused by the strange, cool things people bring in to hawk for money. One guy brought in an 1800's Colt pistol that he had inherited. The world's leading antique arms expert conveniently appeared out of thin air and appraised it at $35,000! After some classic Pawn Stars haggling, they settled on a price of $27,500.

As the closing credits rolled up the screen, the producer asked the seller what he was going to do with the money. He said he would take his family on their first real vacation! My jaw dropped. What a waste of a good, unexpected windfall! First, you should have a family vacation already planned in your budget every year or two. Second, if you master credit card hacking, you don't need to spend $27,500 to go on a world-class vacation. Third, your $27,500 can grow in value and pay you income every year forever if you just invest it! I am not against vacations. Our family has always taken at least one amazing vacation every year. Now we take three! We are only able to take these epic trips because we made investing a priority years ago. So while we get three amazing vacations every year, the pistol guy got one in his whole life. He doesn't prioritize investing and sees unexpected windfalls as money he doesn't deserve to keep and must be immediately spent.

Between work bonuses, birthday cash, and surprise pistol inheritances, it's not unreasonable to think that your family could get a nice chunk of change in unexpected windfalls every year. Let's assume you get an average of $1,200 that you weren't expecting every year for the next seventeen years. If you invest 100% of it and earn the same return as the stock market, your wealth will increase by almost $70,000. So... you could use your $50 birthday gift to go to the movies today, or you could invest it, nurture it for a few years, and help turn your windfalls into $70,000. Use that money to put the down payment on a condo on the beach instead! Now that's a happy birthday!

I've put this concept in this "Exponentiality" section simply because we're not accounting for these unexpected windfalls in our investing plans.

By investing 100% of the money you weren't counting on or projecting to have, you're accelerating your quest to financial independence. In a way, you can look at these investments as infinite from the beginning because the money didn't come out of your 50/40/10 budget. The HACKER method is focused on leveraging the money we receive to grow our wealth, not on the never-ending pursuit of buying more stuff.

HACKER SECTION 5

REVIEW, REWORK, REPEAT & REWARD

CHAPTER 18

REVIEW & REWORK

SEEK CRITIQUE, REWORK THE PLAN & ADJUST STRATEGY

MARKETS REWARD EXCELLENCE WITH CASH.

THE BEST INVESTORS SEEK CRITICISM!

As you work to perfect your investing skills, not only do you need to review your investment performance constantly, more importantly, you need to seek outside feedback. In order to ensure you are getting a complete view of how you are doing and to learn new strategies that can take you further, you need others to help you see your blind spots. In fact, receiving outside criticism of wealth-building is like gasoline to combustible engines: If you don't subject your strategy to critique, your wealth-building vehicle will eventually stall out, and you won't get to your destination. The process of building wealth and of being an investor is actually perfectly suited for the never-ending loop of reviewing, revising, and taking action.

Every investment has a beginning and an exit event. Between buying and selling, most investments also have a stabilization period, and many have a cash flow period. If you're a stock day trader, the whole process from buy to sell could take mere minutes. If you're a buy-and-hold real estate investor like me, a decade could pass from when you purchase to when you sell. Regardless of how long it takes, successful investors constantly seek brutally honest feedback on their portfolio's performance. Plainly said, your success as an investor hinges on your ability to hack into the feedback "review and revise" loop.

Milton Friedman said, "The free market rewards excellence, [and] punishes mediocrity." Expanding on that idea, acting on good feedback is the quickest path to excellence. Ignoring all feedback is the surest path to mediocrity. If receiving hard feedback does not sound fun to you, you are not alone. Most human beings crave reassurance that we're doing well and loathe negative feedback, even if the negative feedback is true. I'm among the worst offenders of this. For as long as I can remember, my default was to hide from criticism. If I couldn't hide, I would reject it altogether. I've found myself ignoring good feedback and, instead, finding ways to discredit the source. It wasn't until I faced a major professional failure that I was forced to learn to seek out hard feedback and take new action.

I'll never forget how I felt the day Mike, my VP of Operations, came into my office and shut the door behind him. We didn't have an appointment, and I could tell by the look on his face that he was upset. Skipping any pleasantries, he said, "Brian, if you don't let the staff run the organization day to day, everyone is going to eventually quit." I had recently gone over his head and barked out some new protocols to some of his team, and he was mad. He went on to say, "We need you out there casting the vision, recruiting workers, and raising money, not creating new policies and procedures all the time. That's my job." From the lens of someone who has a history of struggling to process hard feedback, what I heard him say was, "Brian, you're an awful boss, a terrible manager, a stupid bureaucrat, and an all-around bad person!"

The fight-or-flight instinct kicked in. I decided to fight. I pushed back hard at what he was saying. I had a litany of reasons why I had to keep my fingers on the pulse of the organization. I even found blame in some of the staff he was saying was on the verge of quitting. I told him I was insulted that he would suggest that all I'm good for is raising money, "like an ATM machine or something."

I'm embarrassed to admit three things. First, my insecurity caused me to completely misinterpret his critique as a personal attack. Second, I completely ignored his urgent plea for change, even though he was 100% correct. Third, I continued running things without significant change for several years. Not only did some of my key staff leave as predicted, Mike himself eventually resigned.

Unfortunately for me, I didn't learn the lesson of receiving and processing feedback in a healthy way until it had significantly cost our noble cause to serve others. I can't pretend I've perfected the art of receiving and processing feedback, but I have finally learned the value of it, worked hard to really hear it, and attempted to adjust my strategy accordingly.

Your success in building wealth will hinge on your ability to hear feedback, process it, and then decide on how to adjust your actions and strategies going forward. Not only do you need to hear unsolicited feedback when it comes, you need to proactively seek feedback. Feedback can come in many forms. It could come from your staff, customers or tenants, followers on social media, family or friends, hired consultants, or even from perfect strangers with a fresh perspective.

OVERCOMING THE FEAR OF CRITICISM

Before you can expect to be good at seeking feedback, you must first get over any fear you have. Rather than pretend I am the best one to teach you how to receive feedback, what I can do is alert you to its importance. Therefore, I typically refer people to the book Radical Candor by Kim Scott to get better help in this regard. That said, I do want to share with you the mindset shift that has helped me receive and process feedback.

There is truth in the idiom "a face only a mother could love." Anyone who has started a business or made significant investments can relate to the mother's unconditional love for their baby. Our portfolio (or business, side hustle, etc.) is something we have birthed from our own blood, sweat, and tears. We are so emotionally invested in it that we have a hard time seeing its flaws.

When it comes time to hear or seek feedback, I have learned to emotionally separate myself from the role of founder and metaphorically step outside of my investment strategy. I tell myself that the criticism isn't coming at me like an attack. Rather, I attempt to stand shoulder to shoulder with the person giving me feedback so we are both on the outside looking at the problem together. Picture two people standing next to each other discussing the problems as partners with a genuine quest to find productive solutions. In this scene, there's no animosity and no threats, and we are not coming across as bad people! Some of the best improvements in my life have come from me taking this "outside-looking-in partnership" posture to critical feedback.

DISCERNING WHAT FEEDBACK TO ACT UPON

Once you've learned to partner with your critic, now you need to learn how to discern what feedback you should use to take new action. It's vital that you understand that not all feedback warrants a change on your part. Sometimes, critics have fused personal biases into their perspectives to generate feedback that won't help you grow or succeed. In other cases, certain people may have a personal preference most others will not have.

In our short-term rental business, we have nearly instant feedback from our guests through the five-star feedback system. A couple hours after checkout, our guests receive a request to fill out a brief survey of their experience. Over 96% of our guests rate their experience with us as a 5-star experience. The 4% who rate us as four-star or lower often elaborate on why their score wasn't a five. Even though we get more than 1,000 reviews every year, we read every single one. We try to look at each review from the eyes of the guest and decide on any actions we need to take. It's easy to reject feedback from guests who don't like our decor or furnishings and chalk it up to differing tastes. However, we have learned to pause and ask ourselves hard questions, critical of something as personal as our own design decisions.

There was one instance where we ordered all new living room furniture for a house, based on one particularly negative review that lined up with a couple of other comments from recent guests. We figured that if two or three people agreed, then we needed to act! On the flip side, we once got a one-star review from a lady with a very long list of complaints, culminating in her dismay that our hangers were a mismatch of different colors and styles. We objectively reviewed every single complaint and decided not to act on any of the feedback. We could only assume that either she simply had a unique viewpoint on what was necessary for a short-term rental, or she was taking unrelated stress out on us.

Unfortunately, discerning the difference between good and bad feedback is not black and white. It's really more of an art than a science. It's okay to make a mistake in your decisions based on feedback so long as you are willing to receive it, process it, and then make a decision on what to do with it. At the risk of being repetitive, I'll say again that building wealth is a marathon. You have a lifetime to master the art of responding to feedback. If you're brave enough to work through the process, over time you'll get better and better and know the best response to feedback with more and more ease.

TAKE CORRECTIVE ACTION

Once you've heard, internalized, and processed feedback on your investment strategy, it's time to decide what to do differently and put it into practice. This may sound obvious, but there's a massive graveyard of action plans that died an early death due to a lack of discipline to put them into practice. It's always easier to keep doing what you are comfortable with than to put a good decision into action.

Perhaps the best way to ensure that your decisions are implemented is to seek accountability from the original source of feedback. If that is not practical, recruit someone else to give you the accountability you need. As soon as you have implemented your adjusted strategy, the feedback loop should start all over again. The most successful investors in the world make incremental and constant improvements in their strategy, products, timing, hiring, etc.

Nearly everything in this book encourages you to do things that require constant review, reworking, and then action. The "Hack Your Lifestyle" section is full of fresh ideas that will require tweaks along the way. Your allocation budget will be a living document that needs refreshing every year at a minimum. Your investment strategy is perhaps the most important element to review over and over. And finally, the only way to truly reach exponential growth in your net worth is to review your historical progress and press the gas on the most productive strategies you've deployed. As important as review, rework, and action are, the next step of stepping on the gas on processes that do work is just as important.

CHAPTER 19

REPEAT

RUN THE SAME PLAY UNTIL IT STOPS WORKING

LEARN WHEN TO HOLD 'EM AND WHEN TO FOLD 'EM.

Sweat was pouring off my forehead, dripping into and burning my eyes. My whole body was shaking. I was not sweating or shaking due to exertion. I was scared spitless. I was at our second eighth-grade football practice, and I was the smallest guy on the team. I was so small, I had to cut off pieces of my pads to get them to stop slipping off my skinny shoulders as I ran. Coach lined us up in two rows to run offensive and defensive line drills. With the worst luck imaginable, I was lined up opposite Danny Ault, last year's state wrestling champion! He was a head taller than me, and the smirk on his face showed his brimming confidence. Coach ordered us into the three-point stance facing our opponent, and I had to crane my neck up just to look into his eyes. As soon as our eyes met, I could see he was thrilled. Tossing me around like a rag doll was going to make him look good. I tried to hide my terror.

As coach put his whistle to his lips, I told myself to aim low and put every ounce of my weight, as limited as it was, into Danny's torso. I hoped my low center of gravity would at least keep me from falling on my can. The whistle blew, and I exploded off the line and punched my shoulder into Danny's core with everything I had. When I opened my eyes, it was Danny who was flat on his back. I was stunned, Danny was more stunned, and our coach was thrilled. Coach ran up to us and picked me up from my shoulder pads, asking, "Who is this? Tibbs! You just landed a spot on the front line!"

Then he pulled me to the side and taught me a lesson that not only worked for football, but has served me well in most areas of life. He said, "Tibbs, let your opponent underestimate you, aim low, and explode off the line with all your heart and strength. Do that over and over until your opponent figures it out and it doesn't work anymore. Then you figure out what works next, and you run that play until it stops working. Understand?"

Just as in junior high football, hacking into the wealthy class requires you to figure out which plays work, and then run them over and over until they stop producing the results you want. When something stops working, you have to adjust your approach, find the next formula that works, and run that play over and over until it's no longer productive. Long-term success depends on repeating this cycle over and over. One of the main things that separates people who are successful from those who are not is the dual ability to stay focused on what works and to pivot to another way when the playing field changes.

One of the things that many entrepreneurs struggle with is staying focused. Entrepreneurs are typically dreamers and visionaries. We get bored easily and have a need to be challenged in order to get that adrenaline shot we crave. Many successful investors and business leaders have watched their fortunes falter or even implode simply by messing with the formula that was working perfectly fine. Maybe they started a new product line, went after a new market, or started chasing an unfamiliar customer base. As you break away from the safe and secure life of collecting a paycheck and start creating your own financial destiny, my advice to you is to figure out your niche, work out the formulas that make it successful, and stick with it for the long haul. Building wealth is a marathon, and winning marathons takes an insane amount of commitment to boring repetition as well as adaptation to changing circumstances.

Paradoxically, the other thing many entrepreneurs struggle with is adapting to a changing environment. I understand the contradiction here. On one hand, I'm telling you to run the same boring play over and over; and on the other, I'm saying be ready to throw the play out and run another. You have to learn to identify the times when you need to stay focused and when you need to overhaul. Perhaps one way to look at this focus versus overhaul dance is to realize that the battle to stay focused is within you, and the battle to adapt is coming from the outside. Don't start changing your strategy out of an internal restlessness. However, when the ground under you starts to shift, you need to take a serious look at changing plays.

I have lived through six recessions in my lifetime, and since I started investing twenty-six years ago, I have faced three, including the worst in 100 years with the 2008 credit market meltdown. As importantly, I've lived through the strongest bull market and real estate boom in recent memory. Both bad and good economic times should be considered in the stay-the-course versus change-the-play calculus.

I can think of three key times I changed plays throughout my career. The first play change was when I decided I was going to be a real estate investor. I decided to start buying apartment units every year. I did that for almost ten years. I had a formula and stuck with it until I grew to ten units. Then the whole world changed.

I sensed the market getting too hot in 2005 and 2006. After a long period of hemming and hawing, I decided to change plays and sold 60% of my portfolio, paid off my other buildings, and waited. I missed out on a lot of appreciation in 2005, 2006, and even 2007, but my strategy shift was worth it after real estate crashed in 2008. With this shift, I scooped up steeply discounted property and regrew my portfolio.

I changed plays a third time when I recognized a positive market shift when short-term rentals burst onto the scene. In 2016, my wife and I had seventeen apartment units in Boise, Idaho. I was living overseas and had traveled back to attend to some business in the United States. Even though I owned seventeen homes, they were all rented to tenants, so we stayed in a house that friends of ours made available to us. After eighteen hours of travel from Quito, Ecuador, my exhausted family arrived at the house at one o'clock in the morning. It was pitch black when we walked in the front door. We made it about five feet inside before our tired brains realized that we were walking in about two inches of water! We shut off the water main, called the owner of the house, and by three o'clock in the morning finally crashed at a nearby hotel.

The next morning, I woke up and scanned the cramped hotel room. It looked like my girls had been kicking each other all night as the sheets and comforters were half falling off the bed, and my son had rolled off his blanket and was sleeping with his face mashed into the nasty hotel carpet. Luggage, clothing, shoes, and toys had somehow exploded everywhere to the point that I had to create a pathway to the bathroom. I remember thinking, we can't stay here for three weeks. We have to find another solution. Then my wife suggested, "Hey, maybe we should see if there's a house we could rent on that one site…what's it called?" I replied, "Oh yeah, Airbnb."

I logged on, created an account, and began searching for three-bedroom furnished homes in Boise for three weeks. Always the thrifty shopper, I put the maximum price at $90 per night. I hit "search" and zero results showed up on the screen. I increased the max price to $125. Still nothing! I removed the price minimum, and the cheapest three-bedroom house available for my dates was $165 per night. There were only two other options, both at over $200 per night.

I frustratingly grumbled at how outrageous the price was and how lousy the options were. Then, like a deer in the headlights, I froze. Wait a minute…I have seventeen homes in Boise with an average rent of around $1,000 per month. I did some quick math and figured out that was $33 per night! Thirty days later, I had switched two of my homes to short-term rentals to test the idea. Three months after that, all seventeen were short-term rentals. It's now seven years later, and all thirty-six of my homes are short-term rentals. Ever since we switched to the short-term model, I've tracked what our profits would have been had we stayed with traditional rentals. We're closing in on $1 million in additional profit from short-term over traditional rentals. The day short-term rentals are no longer more profitable than traditional rentals will be the day I have to formulate a new play.

I've heard it said that it takes 10,000 hours to master a craft. If you work forty hours per week for a year and take just two weeks for vacation, you'll put 2,000 hours into your work. That means it can take five years at full-time focus to master something as complex as a market or business strategy. At the beginning of a new play, the effort required to make it function is much higher than it is once you've mastered that play. Just another reason to only shift plays when the upside is big enough or the downside is rough enough to justify it. As you learn the art and science of building serious wealth, fight your internal restlessness to stay focused and keep one eye on major shifting trends to ensure that you can keep climbing.

CHAPTER 20

I'M HERE FOR MY REWARD

YOU WENT. YOU SAW. YOU CONQUERED.

I'M HERE FOR MY REWARD!

My question is not if any readers of this book skipped to this chapter first, but how many. Like all biological beings, most of our actions are ultimately executed for the hope or expectation of a reward at some point in the process. Because of this reward-centric nature, weight-loss programs highly emphasize the skinny, pretty people going out on dates with other skinny, pretty people. They don't highlight the scene from twelve months prior of a chubby guy slogging away on the treadmill while staring adoringly at the irresistible Krispy Kreme donuts across the room. Most wealth creation gurus do the same thing in showcasing the guy in a custom suit standing out front of his private jet and Lamborghini with the skinny girl from the diet ad at his side. They are less than forthcoming on the immense amount of work and focus it takes to accumulate the level of wealth that affords such a lifestyle.

If you just cracked this book open and started here, please continue on to read the chapter and allow your mind to race with the possibilities of a life of significant wealth. One of the first steps in building wealth is to visualize yourself at this place anyway, so it can actually be motivational. However, I can confidently predict that the reward step will likely be the hardest step for you. As counterintuitive as it sounds, let me attempt to explain the psychology that happens when you build significant wealth over time.

As we have discussed throughout this book, an individual who acquires significant wealth transforms into a person constantly measuring return on investment. They see every dollar spent on consumer stuff (like private jets and fast cars) as not only money spent and lost forever, but money that can no longer be used to make more money. For some multimillionaires, spending money actually conjures up negative emotions and feelings. Let that sink in for a minute.

If you truly learn to follow the HACKER method closely, I would be willing to bet that your goal line will continually move further away each time you reach a goal. You'll arrive at a certain benchmark, enjoy the thrill for a day or so, then set a new higher goal and start marching for it. While I don't discourage striving for ever higher goals, I do want to warn you against ignoring this part of the "R" step in HACKER. People who are incapable of accepting their reward for their labor have an unhealthy relationship with money and/or wealth. People who have an unhealthy relationship with money are almost always miserable and/or depressed.

Unfortunately, I didn't learn the discipline of "reward" until relatively recently. In fact, I didn't spend a dime of the money created by my investments until I was a multimillionaire. The year our net worth crossed $4 million, my family spent less than $38,000 in living expenses. That included eating out, rent, vacations, groceries…everything. Yes, rent.

Our family of five was paying $1,000 per month for an 850-square-foot apartment that year. We held title to seventeen homes, but were renting a tiny apartment. Even as I write this, I can hardly believe how strict I was with our family finances. I'm embarrassed, actually. Money is OUR tool to use and doesn't deserve to enslave us. For too long, I didn't follow my own 50/40/10 budget rule. As the investment income increased, I just poured it all back into future investments. There were stretches of time where 70% of our income was invested.

After a lot of thought and not a little bit of therapy, I'm happy to share that I've started to learn how to enjoy the fruits of my labor. I guess proof might be that the last apartment our whole family lived in could comfortably fit in my master bedroom today. To get there, however, we had to change our language around the use of our money. Instead of using the negative word "spending," we now ask ourselves how much money we can and should "harvest." There's not a farmer in the world who would work hard all summer raising crops only to skip the harvest season. If we aren't harvesting some of our fruit, we're missing a fundamental aspect of life. As with everything in the HACKER method, we've created systems that govern how much of our estate we "harvest."

THE HARVEST:REWARD FORMULA

The average American is taught to work hard for their productive decades and "save up enough for retirement." Then, when they reach that magic age of 65 (or is it 67? Or 70? It keeps getting older), they stop earning a paycheck and start tapping into their "retirement nest egg." Almost all traditional "financial advisors" will consult their clients to estimate how many years they expect to live in order to know how much retirement runway they need. Not only is it morbid to guess when you'll die, it's an absurdly futile exercise. Nobody can predict how long they'll live. What happens if you guess you'll die much later than you do? Or worse, what happens if you guess you'll die much sooner than you do? I've seen painful examples in my own extended family of both scenarios.

The chart below shows the typical financial advisor retirement model. This assumes your working years' salary is steadily increasing. It also assumes you are always automatically socking away 10% of your salary into a retirement account and earning an average of 9% returns until you retire at 70. After retirement, your advisor will shift your investments to a much more conservative portfolio, dramatically slowing your returns.

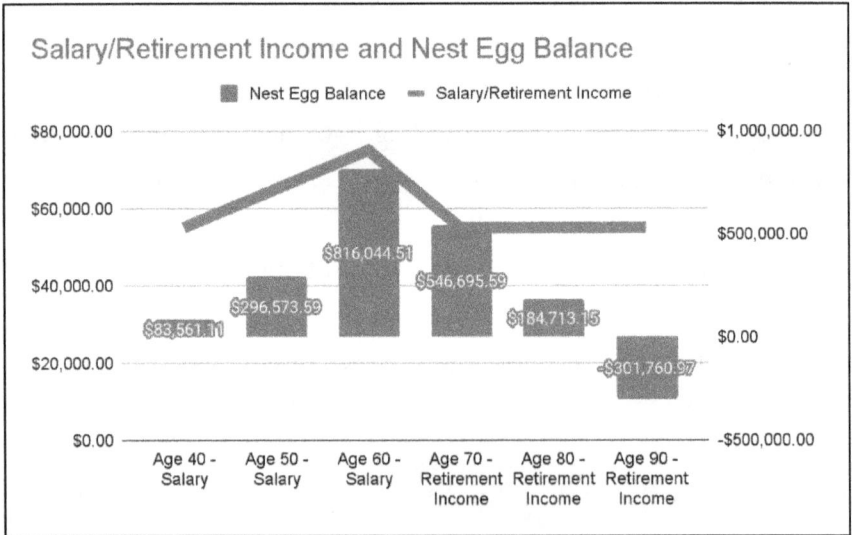

Salary/Retirement Income and Nest Egg Balance

Legend: Nest Egg Balance — Salary/Retirement Income

$83,561.11	$296,573.59	$816,044.51	$546,695.59	$184,713.15	-$301,760.97
Age 40 - Salary	Age 50 - Salary	Age 60 - Salary	Age 70 - Retirement Income	Age 80 - Retirement Income	Age 90 - Retirement Income

Left axis: $0.00, $20,000.00, $40,000.00, $60,000.00, $80,000.00
Right axis: -$500,000.00, $0.00, $500,000.00, $1,000,000.00

In this model, if you plan to live to ninety, upon retiring—to ensure you don't run out of money—your income has to drop from $75,000 to $55,000 annually without adjustments for future inflation. That's what you were making three decades prior! If you live to 100, you'll run out of the nest egg completely. What are you supposed to do at age ninety-two when you have no money? This model not only forces you to live on less money, but your hard-earned nest egg begins to dissolve before your eyes at a rapid clip. There goes the inheritance for your children.

The HACKER method is the opposite of the traditional financial advisor concept. You don't have to predict your death, and you don't need to wait until some magic age to start harvesting. Instead, your wealth should continue to grow until the end of life, leaving an ever-expanding estate to your heirs, community, church, or favorite charity.

I lay out my harvesting formula below. However, you may be starting the game earlier or later than me. Or you may have different end goals from mine. Regardless, I encourage you to think critically about your own situation and adapt this formula to fit your personal situation.

First, it's important to recognize that there are two types of crops that we harvest from. The first type of crop we can harvest from is our overall estate, or our net worth, which resides on the balance sheet. I'm talking about the wealth stored up in assets like buildings, financial securities, retirement accounts, reserve cash, etc. The second type of crop would be the cash flows from those estate assets. This money shows up on the profit and loss statement in the form of rental cash flow, stock dividends, business profits, royalties, and profits from sold assets. It's important to distinguish the two because both have very different effects on your future.

Up until now, the 40% investing account was untouchable for personal expenditures. As we start to harvest, I suggest opening yourself up to using some of your investment account, but only to purchase assets that have the potential to increase in value—namely, your personal home. Taking a few hundred thousand dollars out of a multimillion-dollar estate to purchase a home is reasonable and enables you to begin to live that abundant life you've been working so hard to obtain. I would, however, discourage you from using any of your investing account for anything consumable or for assets that depreciate, like vehicles. You don't want your investment account to stop growing in value.

I also suggest you adjust your 50/40/10 formula once your assets are generating at least as much income as your salary from your job. This will enable you to quit your job without taking a smaller income.

Let's say you have acquired $10,000,000 in assets, and hold $5,000,000 in debt secured on those assets for a net worth of $5,000,000. A 4% increase in asset values in a year will add $400,000 to your net worth. At that point, your 40% investment deposit is a small contributor to your net worth, but a huge drag on your income.

If you were to adjust your 50/40/10 budget to 70/20/10, your spending budget would actually be higher even after quitting your salaried job. The chart below illustrates the diminishing impact of investing your income back into your enterprise after reaching a significant net worth. Here we are assuming three things. First, you maintain no more than 50% of your net worth in debt. Second, your assets are appreciating at an average rate of 4% and your cash flows equal 3% of your equity. Finally, we are assuming you quit your salaried job after reaching $4 million in net worth.

Total Assets	$2,000,000	$3,000,000	$6,000,000	$8,000,000	$10,000,000
Total Debt	$1,000,000	$1,500,000	$3,000,000	$4,000,000	$5,000,000
Net Worth	**$1,000,000**	**$1,500,000**	**$3,000,000**	**$4,000,000**	**$5,000,000**
4% Asset Appreciation	*$80,000*	*$120,000*	*$240,000*	*$320,000*	*$400,000*
Cash Flows (3% of Equity)	$30,000	$45,000	$90,000	$120,000	$150,000

Salary from Job	$80,000	$80,000	$80,000	$0	$0
Total Income	$110,000	$125,000	$170,000	$120,000	$150,000
Allocation Budget Splits	50/40/10	50/40/10	50/40/10	70/20/10	70/20/10
Spending Budget	$55,000	$62,500	$85,000	$84,000	$105,000
Investing Budget	**$44,000**	**$50,000**	**$68,000**	**$24,000**	**$30,000**
Charity	$11,000	$12,500	$17,000	$12,000	$15,000
Investment Allocation to Asset appreciation ratio	55.00%	41.67%	28.33%	7.50%	7.50%

Once you have reached a certain net worth, the sacrifices you made early in the journey are what create the returns you are enjoying today. If you were to continue to stick with the 50/40/10 fund split, the 40% investment fund would have a very small effect on your net worth growth. On the other hand, shifting half of that 40% to your spending will have a dramatically positive effect on your lifestyle.

Enjoy the abundance that has been entrusted to you, stay humble, and start thinking about what you want your legacy to be. Which brings me to the final part of our wealth-hacking journey: the morality of wealth.

PART 3

THE MORALITY OF WEALTH

CHAPTER 21

THE INTERSECTION OF WEALTH, RELATIONSHIPS, & DUTY

WHAT GOOD IS IT FOR A MAN TO GAIN THE WHOLE WORLD, YET FORFEIT THEIR SOUL?

Every nerve in my body was on high alert. I had just asked them for $1,000,000. Now that I had let those words come out of my mouth, all of my energy was going toward concealing my intense discomfort and anxiety. We just sat there in an awkward pause for a few seconds that seemed like hours. They looked at each other without saying anything. Then they both looked at me, and she said, "We need to pray about it, and we'll get back to you. But regardless of whether we give you the million dollars or not, we just want to say thank you for the opportunity." I left their home in a fog, trying to process all that had just happened.

To bring you up to speed, I was raising money for our non-profit organization for an upcoming campaign to serve some of the poorest communities in Ecuador. These two lovely people were long-time friends and had been generous donors in the past. I had never asked them for this much money, however, and I was scared to death. In the end, they decided not to give the full million, although they still made a six-figure donation to help us get started. What stands out to me about this story is not the dollar amount, the generosity, or the disappointment of not raising the full amount, but how they responded when I asked them for $1,000,000. "Thank you for the opportunity…" What?! I have two questions. First, why would anyone thank someone else for an opportunity to give away money for nothing tangible in return? Second, why was I so surprised at their response? Let's explore both questions.

I think the answer to the first question can be summed up in one word: gratitude. This couple is grateful for the great fortune they have been blessed with in their lives. They were entrusted with a significant financial fortune, but that is not the only fortune they have. They also have children, grandchildren, their church, their business partners, their neighbors, and a myriad of non-profit causes that they LOVE to support. They have lived a fruitful life, and their greatest joy as they age is just to be thankful for all they have and use it to have the biggest possible impact. They appreciate it when trustworthy people give them opportunities to have a big impact. For them, writing checks is easy. It's finding capable managers of their money that's the hard part.

Having raised over $20,000,000 for my non-profit, my experience with this couple is actually the rule rather than the exception. Almost everyone I approached was thankful for the fact that I invited them to be a part of the movement. What's crazy to me is that I never really expected a response so full of gratitude. Which leads me to my second question. Why does their gratitude surprise me?

Money is not alive. Money has no feelings. Money has no soul. Yet money elicits an emotional reaction in most humans on a level with how we respond to other humans who are alive and do have feelings and a soul. I guess this is true because in our modern society, we need money in order to meet our most basic needs. Which of Mazlow's basic human needs can we obtain without money? Unless you are a mountain recluse, it takes money to get shelter, food, and water. Therefore, our very survival depends on money.

Stemming from our survival dependency on money, our culture has certain beliefs around money that powerfully impact our view of and reaction to money. One of those cultural rules is NOT to talk about money! As CEO of the non-profit, one of my primary roles was to cultivate the larger donations we needed to succeed at our mission. In other words, I HAD to talk about money. Not only did I have to talk about money, but I had to talk to wealthy people about them giving me their money! That task breaks just about every unspoken cultural rule around the topic of money. If I had to guess, you're probably saying to yourself, "Yeah, I would hate a job where I had to ask people for money!" We feel that way because we have accepted some mistaken cultural ideas around money.

In this final part of the book, I want to inspire you to break free from the dark side of money and the process of building wealth. I want to steer you away from the stereotypical image of the rich guy standing in front of insanely expensive cars, and plant in your heart the desire to be like the wealthy couple who is thankful to be able to give away vast sums of their fortune to make the world a better place. I want you to experience the incredible rush of writing large checks to support the cause that makes your heart beat and your mind race. I want the people who know you best to first describe you as kind and generous before they describe you as rich. I want your funeral to be packed and filled with stories of how you improved people's lives.

My perspective on money is molded by my Judeo-Christian worldview. While I am constantly striving to reflect all of the ideals around money and wealth, I am the first to confess that I often fall short. Nonetheless, I want to share with you the three pillars that I stand on as I continue to build wealth. Simply put, if you follow these ideals, your soul will grow more beautiful, you'll feel more gratitude, and your life will have an infinitely higher impact than if you seek wealth simply to acquire a bigger house, a faster car, and that private jet.

MORALITY OF WEALTH PILLAR #1 - WELL DONE GOOD AND FAITHFUL SERVANT

There's a passage in the Bible in Matthew chapter 25 where Jesus is telling a parable. Parables are made-up stories that teach a principal. This particular story is called the Parable of the Talents. A talent, for those of you not current on your ancient Roman exchange rates, would be a bag of gold roughly equivalent to twenty years' wages for a common worker of the time. Since a perfect exchange rate is impossible, let's keep the math simple and say twenty years' wages is worth $50,000 per year for twenty years, which is $1,000,000. A modernized title of this story could be the Parable of Ten Million Dollars. I point this out to show that the parable is not talking about an insignificant amount of money here.

This story consists of a business owner and his three money managers. The business owner is going on a trip and is placing huge sums of money in each of the manager's hands to invest on his behalf. His instructions are to grow the wealth and then give a report of how they did when he returns. We don't know how much he wants them to make, and we don't know how long he'll be away. The business owner gives five talents ($5,000,000) to the first manager, two talents ($2,000,000) to the second, and one talent ($1,000,000) to the third.

The first manager gets to work investing the money. He doubles his $5 million to $10 million! I don't care who you are and I don't really care how long it took him, but it takes incredible skill to double any amount of money. His accomplishment is impressive. The second manager takes his $2 million and doubles it as well. Again, a very impressive result. The third manager is crippled by fear, however. He takes his $1 million into his backyard, digs a giant hole in the middle of the night, and buries it! If I had to guess, his fear of losing even part of the money was so great that he would rather return the full amount without a gain than have to admit to investing poorly and losing the owner's money.

The business owner returns and asks for the accounting report from each person. The first guy hands over $10 million, the second guy $4 million, and the last guy $1 million, conceivably still with a little bit of dirt stuck to the gold. The business owner praises the first two guys by saying one of the most famous quotes in the Bible, "Well done, good and faithful servant!" He then continues by saying, "Now enter into the joy of your master." Many theologians translate the "joy of the master" to be heaven.

The business owner then turns to the third manager and harshly scolds him, saying, "You wicked, lazy servant…you should have put my money on deposit with the bankers, so that when I returned I would have received it back with interest." Then he says, "Throw that worthless servant outside, into the darkness, where there will be weeping and gnashing of teeth." Theologians translate that place to be hell!

Knowing what I know about Jesus, I cannot honestly conclude that Jesus wants us to dedicate our lives solely to the quest of building massive wealth. What I can confidently deduce, however, is that Jesus wants us to be shrewd, effective managers of all that we have. He wants us to leverage our money, possessions, relationships, bodies, minds, and hearts to the maximum. He wants us to grow, take risks, be bold, be successful, be creative, be responsible.

I honestly think the third manager would still have been allowed into the joy of the master had he attempted to grow his wealth and failed. The point was to make an effort and not to be lazy or ruled by fear. If that is the case, this story is to inspire us to take risks, measure our success, try again, and constantly try to improve. We can rest knowing the balance of our account is not the point. The guy with $10,000,000 and the guy with $4,000,000 both received the same percentage reward. They were equally rewarded because they took risks and maximized what they were entrusted with.

The bottom line of Pillar #1 for us today is:

- **We were meant to be EXTREMELY successful!** - Humans thrive when they meet the challenge of maximizing what they have. We are creative and adaptable. We sense great satisfaction when we accomplish hard things. Therefore, the challenge of growth is vital to our happiness and soul. Growth of wealth, relationships, experiences - it all fits into the larger picture of being successful and effective people.
- Humans who cower in fear and never take risks are likely to live a more miserable existence. One could argue that the person who refuses to take risks is actually greedier than the one who is willing to release their grip on money and take risks.
- It is not a sin to seek wealth. It is a sin, however, to put such a high value on money that you lock it away where it can't be used or be invested.

MORALITY OF WEALTH PILLAR #2 - CHASING AFTER THE WIND

Hopefully, we've accepted the idea that building wealth is not bad or not something that stains our human soul. That said, it's vital that we establish the counterbalance to Pillar #1. The premise of the second pillar teaches us not to build wealth for the sake of being wealthy. In other words, we should not love our money above all else. It's an easy trap to fall into. As investors, we put a ton of energy and focus into multiplying our resources. When so much time and energy go toward one thing, it's easy to get obsessed with wealth and even "fall in love" with money. The emotional connections to success can easily lead to an unhealthy relationship with money.

I have adopted this pillar from several passages in the Old Testament book of Ecclesiastes. The simplest example is found in chapter 2, verse 26, which says, "To the person who pleases him, God gives wisdom, knowledge, and happiness, but to the sinner he gives the task of gathering and storing up wealth to hand it over to the one who pleases God. This too is meaningless, a chasing after the wind."

Imagine for a moment chasing wind. It's immediately understood to be a futile exercise. The author of this ancient wisdom is saying that building and storing up wealth is like chasing wind. The concept here is that if wealth itself becomes the motivation and the only thing that matters, you're wasting your time. My experience working with very wealthy people is that the ones who have an imbalanced focus on wealth alone are miserable. They don't have many friends and spend an insane amount of time focusing on making money. Their mood shifts up and down based on their investment performance.

If you've ever heard the phrase, "money is the root of all evil," you've heard a misquote. The Bible actually says, "The love of money is the root of all evil." As we see with Pillar #1, money itself is not evil. Loving money is.

The bottom line of Pillar #2 is:

- As you learn how to live Pillar #1, don't let your heart fall in love with wealth itself.
- As your wealth grows, make sure you use your wealth as a tool to make our world a better place.
- Material possessions are not eternal, so don't let yourself be fooled that the acquisition of those materials increases the value of your soul at all.

MORALITY OF WEALTH PILLAR #3 - I SHALL NOT SACRIFICE WHAT ISN'T MINE

Pillar #3 is the perfect synthesis of Pillars 1 and 2. Pillar #3 is based on a biblical story of King Solomon. If we accept the Bible's account of King Solomon's wealth, he would be worth approximately $2.9 trillion today. That is more than ten times wealthier than the richest person alive now. There is a specific story where someone wanting to gain favor with Solomon offers to donate his livestock so that Solomon would not have to use his own livestock for the sacrifice. Solomon grows angry and declares that he refuses to sacrifice that which is not his. He had the wisdom and discipline to make the sacrifice himself so that he would be able to feel the effect. He knew the act of giving from his wealth was vital to the health of his soul and an action that his God required.

Perhaps the greatest misery on earth is to live like Ebenezer Scrooge before he was visited by the three ghosts of Christmas past, present, and future. Conversely, the greatest joy on earth is to live like the version of Scrooge after his paranormal experience.

As we have discussed in the chapter on the 50/40/10 budget, it's vital that we grow our generosity muscles from the very beginning by separating 10% to give away. To refuse to be generous is to violate Pillar #2 and place such a high value on money that we cannot part with it. Additionally, refusing to be generous robs us of the joy that can only come from doing something truly selfless that helps other people and our world.

Most religions teach a concept that promises that being good will reap good. Whether or not there's a supernatural effect here or not is irrelevant. Truth is, being generous has a tendency to bring rewards in many ways to the generous person.

The bottom line of Pillar #3 is:

- Find real joy by loosening your grip on at least 10% of your wealth to give away to causes that seek to leave the world in a better place than you found it.
- Your failure to be generous will bring misery because you will violate Pillar #2
- Being generous is a part of Pillar #1 in that you are responsible to not only grow your own personal wealth, but improve the world around you as much as you can.
- Your generosity has a tendency to pay you dividends in many ways. Letting go of some of your wealth can sometimes increase your wealth in ways you don't expect.

Make as much money as you can. Love your family, your neighbors, and your world more than you love money. Generously give your money away to make the world a better place. Hear the words, "Well done, good and faithful servant."

SOURCES REFERENCED

https://www.statista.com/statistics/456925/
median-size-of-single-family-home-usa/.

https://compasscaliforniablog.com/
have-american-homes-changed-much-over-the-years-take-a-look/

https://www.mortgagecalculator.org/helpful-advice/
american-mortgage-history.

https://www.bankrate.com/retirement/retirement-plan-calculator/
https://www.mortgagecalculator.org/helpful-advice/american-
mortgage-history.php

https://www.forbes.com/advisor/credit-cards/history-of-credit-cards/

https://shiftprocessing.com/cash-vs-credit-card-spending-statistics/

https://www.opportunityatlas.org

https://rajchetty.com/publications/

https://docs.iza.org/dp1938.pdf

https://www.moneygeek.com/credit-cards/analysis/average-credit-card-debt/

S&P calculator: https://dqydj.com/sp-500-periodic-reinvestment-calculator-dividends/

Federal Reserve of St. Louis https://fred.stlouisfed.org

US Bureau of Labor Statistics https://data.bls.gov/

Freddie Mac https://www.freddiemac.com/

https://www.scientificamerican.com/article/why-some-people-spend-more-impulsively-during-tough-economic-times/

https://www.creditdonkey.com/lottery-winner-statistics.html

https://www.bankrate.com/retirement/retirement-plan-calculator/

Volkswagen Golf Dimensions 2022 - Length, Width, Height, Turning Circle, Ground Clearance, Wheelbase & Size | CarsGuide

Dodge Ram 3500 Length (2002 - 2022) (autopadre.com)

Toyota Highlander Hybrid Depreciation (caredge.com)

What Is the Best Age and Mileage for a Used Car? | U.S. News

How Much Do Uber Drivers Make In 2023? | Ridester.com

https://thesavvycouple.com/get-paid-to-advertise-on-your-car/

https://www.investopedia.com/financial-edge/0110/10-things-to-know-about-1031-exchanges.aspx

https://www.nasdaq.com/articles/money-printing-and-inflation%3A-covid-cryptocurrencies-and-more

https://wallethub.com/edu/cc/number-of-credit-cards/25532

https://www.fool.com/the-ascent/personal-finance/articles/heres-a-breakdown-of-americans-monthly-credit-card-bills/

https://www.consumerfinance.gov/about-us/blog/americans-pay-120-billion-in-credit-card-interest-and-fees-each-year/

https://upgradedpoints.com/credit-cards/credit-card-facts-statistics-debt-spending/

https://www.bostonfed.org/publications/research-data-report/2017/the-2016-diary-of-consumer-payment-choice.aspx

RealtyMogul.com™ | Famous Real Estate Investing Quotes

Andrew Carnegie | Biography, Company, Steel, Philanthropy, Books, & Facts | Britannica

Real Estate Meaning | Origin, Etymology, History, and Definition (fastexpert.com)

Voting Rights in the United States: Timeline - HISTORY

What is the Average Compensation For 9/11 Victims | VCF Claims (wtcvictimfund.com)

1950 Census Records: A Window to History

https://www.worlddata.info/america/usa/inflation-rates.php#:~:text=During%20the%20observation%20period%20from,year%20inflation%20rate%20was%204.0%25.

https://www.fancypantshomes.com/celebrity-homes/warren-buffett-house-in-omaha/

https://www.scientificamerican.com/article/why-some-people-spend-more-impulsively-during-tough-economic-times/

ABOUT THE AUTHOR

As Brian Tibbs emerged into young adulthood, it was clear to himself and everyone around him that he was destined to be a businessman. By age twenty-six, he had already started investing in real estate, was an executive in his dad's financial services company and co-owner of another small online retailer.

But Brian felt a calling down a different path. Over the next three years, Brian married Jill Bramhall, resigned from his father's company, sold his online business and liquidated 60% of his real estate portfolio and moved, sight unseen, to Guatemala.

Over the course of the next sixteen years, Brian built a team that ended up recruiting and training 380 leaders to plant ninety-six churches in eleven countries. They raised over $20,000,000 for the cause and built over 150,000 sq. ft of churches and related facilities.

Brian and his family made very little money as missionaries. Dividing their total ministry salary into the total hours both Brian and Jill worked over the sixteen years in ministry shows that they made just $9.20 per hour, below the legal minimum wage in most states.

Their modest salary forced them to create a wealth building philosophy that didn't require a big paycheck. Living under this financial constraint is how the HACKER Method, which is thoroughly detailed in this book, was discovered and implemented. The HACKER Method enabled the Tibbs' to create a multi-million dollar net worth by Brian's forty-fourth birthday.

Although Brian has retired from full time missionary work, his desire to serve others remains a primary focus. He launched The Unexpected Investor with the singular goal to help other people who also feel financially constrained, transform themselves into wealthy, powerful and generous investors using the HACKER Method.

Brian is fluent in Spanish and conversational in Portuguese. He earned a Bachelor's degree in Business Administration with an emphasis in Finance. He later earned a Master's degree in Christian Apologetics from Liberty University and has several organizational leadership certificates, including one from Harvard Business School.